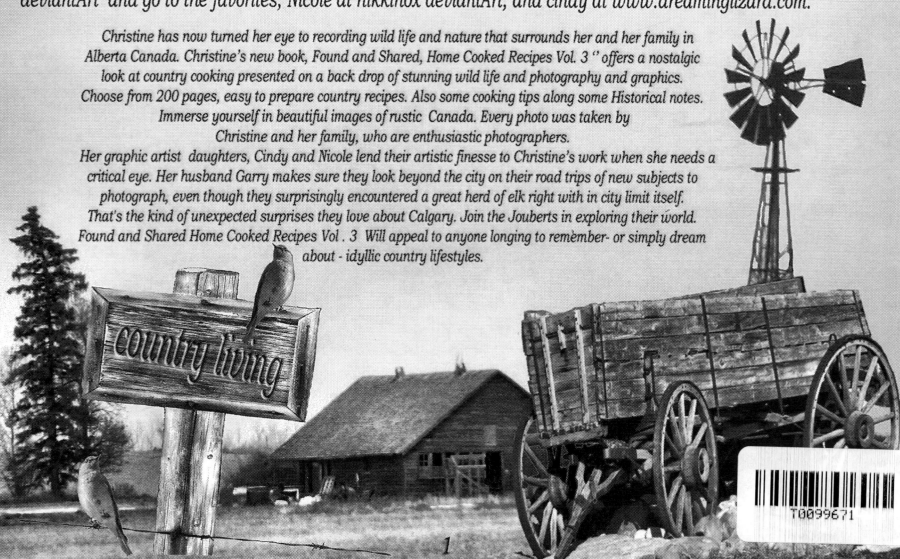

Paintsculpturist Christine Joubert has recorded a legacy of Calgary's historic sandstone buildings, many which no longer exist. Preserving a bit of the city's history was a labor of love she felt was important. Her "SANDSTONE CITY" collection of 18 paintings, incorporating actual sandstone from one of the buildings, captures it perfectly. If you wish to see these works of art they can be seen on the internet at Prairiestone on deviantArt and go to the favorites, Nicole at nikkinox deviantArt, and cindy at www.dreaminglizard.com.

Christine has now turned her eye to recording wild life and nature that surrounds her and her family in Alberta Canada. Christine's new book, Found and Shared, Home Cooked Recipes Vol. 3 " offers a nostalgic look at country cooking presented on a back drop of stunning wild life and photography and graphics. Choose from 200 pages, easy to prepare country recipes. Also some cooking tips along some Historical notes. Immerse yourself in beautiful images of rustic Canada. Every photo was taken by Christine and her family, who are enthusiastic photographers.

Her graphic artist daughters, Cindy and Nicole lend their artistic finesse to Christine's work when she needs a critical eye. Her husband Garry makes sure they look beyond the city on their road trips of new subjects to photograph, even though they surprisingly encountered a great herd of elk right with in city limit itself. That's the kind of unexpected surprises they love about Calgary. Join the Jouberts in exploring their world. Found and Shared Home Cooked Recipes Vol . 3 Will appeal to anyone longing to remember- or simply dream about - idyllic country lifestyles.

country living

1

Appetizers

My Photo/ 08

2

Devil's Dip

Saute 1/4 cup sliced mushrooms, 1/4 cup chopped celery, 1/4 cup chopped onion in 3 tb margarine until soft but not browned. Add 1 can mushroom soup, 1 pkg. frozen chopped broccoli, cooked and drained and 1 6 oz. pkg. garlic cheese, cut small pieces stirring constantly, until cheese is melted and blended. Add a dash of hot sauce. Pour into a serving dish and serve with corn chips

Vegetable Dip

Combine 1 cup mayonnaise, 1 cup catsup, 1/3 cup lemon juice, 1 tb. dry mustard, 2 tb. drained horseradish, 1 tb. sugar, 1/2 tsp. Worcestershire sauce, salt and pepper to taste and mix well. Chill until thickened. Serve with fresh cut vegetables.

Hot Cheese Puffs

Preheat oven at 400. Cream 1 cup shredded Cheddar Cheese, 3 tb. soft butter, blend in 1/2 cup flour, 1 tsp paprika, 1/2 tsp. Worcestershire sauce, dash of cayenne pepper and salt to taste. Mold 1 tsp. dough around each of 24 medium stuffed olives. Place on a ungreased cookie sheet. Bake for 12 minutes or until golden brown. You may substitute with walnuts, pecans, or cocktail frankfurters

Hot Cheese Dunk

Stir 1 can cheddar cheese soup until smooth, blend in 2 tb. catsup, 1/8 tsp. powder oregano, 1/8 tsp. garlic and 1/8 tsp onion powder. Heat, stirring frequently. Dunk bread or toast squares.

Garry's Photo

3

Hawaiian Meatballs

Drain 1 8oz. can pineapple tidbits and reserve pineapple juice. Place pineapple on paper towel to drain. Soak 3 slices bread in a small amount of water, and squeeze out moister. Mix 1 lb. lean ground beef with the bread, 1 egg, 1 tsp onion salt and mix well, shape into balls, enclosing a pineapple tidbit in each ball. Brown slowly in 3 tb. margarine and 2 tb. oil, shaking pan to keep balls round and to brown evenly,

Add water to reserved pineapple juice to make 1/2 cup if needed. Blend juice with 3/4 cup beef broth, 2 tb. lemon juice, 3 tb. catsup and 2 tsp. cornstarch in a small sauce pan, Pour over meat balls. Cook over moderate heat for 10 minutes or until sauce boils and thickens slightly. Serve hot in a chafing dish. Makes 30 meatballs.

3

My Photos/09

PO PO Meat Balls

Mix 1/2 lb. ground beef, 1/2 tsp. salt, 1 tsp. chilli powder, 1 tsp. dry mustard, 1/2 tsp. dried rosemary and 1 egg just to blend lightly. Form into 3/4 inch balls. Saute lightly in butter, roll in grated Parmesan cheese. Insert on a water soaked wooden long pick onto each ball. Toast over a BBQ or a charcoal hibachi until browned and cooked through.

Chick Pea Dip

Puree 1 can chick peas in a blender. Mix in 1/2 cup pulverized sesame seeds, 2 tb. lemon juice, 6 tb, water in blender until the consistency of ground nuts. Stir in 1 cup cold water. Add to chick peas, stirring until smooth, add 1 clove garlic diced fine, 2 tb. olive oil, and 1/2 tsp salt. Mix to incorporate well. Sprinkle with 1 tsp. parsley flakes. Serve with chunks of bread or crackers.

Deviled Eggs

Have 6 hard cooked eggs halved lengthwise and yolks removed. Mash egg yolks with fork, add 2 tb. mayonnaise, 1/2 tsp. salt, 1/4 tsp. pepper, 1 tb, chopped sweet pickle and 1 tsp. finely chopped onion, blend well. Fill egg whites. Garnish with a sprinkle of paprika.

Stuffed Pickles

Blend 1 3 oz. pkg cream cheese, 2 tb. salad dressing, 1 tb. Worcestershire sauce and 1/2 cup chopped walnuts until smooth. Stuff 3 large cored dill pickle centers. Chill for 1 hour or until cheese is firm. Slice crosswise.

MY Photo/09

4

Salads

Vegetables

Soups

Iceberg , Green Pea Salad

With Thyme Dressing

Combine 1/3 cup salad oil, 2 tb. white wine vinegar, 1 small minced clove of garlic, 2 tsp. Dijon mustard, 1/2 tsp. thyme, 1/2 tsp. sugar, salt and pepper. Cover and refrigerate for 1 hour.

Mix together 1 head Iceberg lettuce ripped into bite size pieces, 2/3 cup sliced celery, 1 thinly slice small red onion, 1 pkg. 10 oz. thawed frozen peas.. Pour over dressing and toss lightly, garnish with 3 hard cooked eggs cut in wedges.

Garrys Photo/09

6

Coleslaw

Finely shred 8 cups of cabbage,
Place in a large salad bowl.
In another bowl mix together
1 cup mayonnaise,
4 tb. Dijon mustard,
2 tb. dill pickle juice,
2/3 cup very finely chopped onion, mix well.
Toss with cabbage until thoroughly mixed.
Cover and refrigerate for 1 hour before serving.

My Photo/07

Fruit & Rice Salad

Combine 1 1/2 cup cooked rice, 3 cups unpeeled and diced apples, 1 cup drained crushed pineapple, 2 cups miniature marshmallows add 1/2 cup sugar, 1/4 tsp. salt, 1/2 tsp. vanilla, 1/2 cup chopped walnuts and mix well. Top with whipped cream or with a dessert topping mix.

8

Beef & Barley Salad

Mix 1 cup cooked pearl barley, 1/4 lb. roast beef, cut into strips, 1/4 cup thinly sliced green onions, 3 cherry tomatoes cut in quarters, 2 tb. fresh chopped flat leaf parsley and 2 tb. golden raisins, set aside.

In a small sauce pan combine 1 tb. red wine vinegar, 1 tb. Dijon mustard, 2 tsp. olive oil, 1 1/2 tsp. firmly packed brown sugar, 1 1/2 tsp. lemon juice and 1 1/2 tsp. water with a dash of salt and pepper. Cook over medium heat, stirring occasionally, until mixture comes to a boil until sugar has dissolved. Remove and pour over salad, toss to coat and serve or cover and chill. (2 servings 300 cal.)

9

Garrys Photo

Caesar Salad

In a large bowl rub 1 clove of garlic over the inside surface of bowl, discard garlic. Add 4 cups torn romaine lettuce leaves toss and set aside.

In a small bowl combine 2 tb. water, 2 chopped anchovy fillets, 1 tb. lemon juice, 1 tb. red wine vinegar, 2 tsp. Dijon mustard, 2 tsp. olive oil, 1/2 tsp. Worcestershire sauce and mix thoroughly and set aside. In a heat resistant bowl add 1 unshelled egg, slowly pour boiling water over to cover. Let stand for 3 minutes, drain water. Crack egg into bowl and beat slightly, add to lettuce along with anchovy mixture, toss to mix thoroughly coat. Toss with croutons, sprinkle with grated Parmesan. (2 servings, 222 cal.)

Garry's Photo/08

Low cal Turkey Citrus Salad

Toss 1 cup turkey cut in cubes with 1 cup grapefruit sections, 1/2 cup orange sections, 1 head lettuce cut up in bite size pieces, coated with a low cal dressing and toss until well coated. serves 2.

My Photos/07

Stuffed Tomato Cottage Cheese Salad

Combine 1 pint small curd low fat cottage cheese, 1/2 cup finely chopped green onion, 1/2 cup chopped celery, 1/4 cup chopped red bell pepper 1/2 cup shredded carrot, 1/4 cup chopped radishes, 1/2 tsp. each of garlic salt, dry mustard and dill weed. Cover and chill 1 hour or until next day to blend. To serve cut 2 tomatoes in half and scoop out seeds and pulp place half on each plate, fill each with equal portion of cottage cheese mixture, sprinkle with paprika.

12

My Photo/ 10

Avocado & Celery Toss

In a bowl combine 1/2 cup mayonnaise,
2 tb. Dijon mustard. Add salt and pepper
to taste, 2 large peeled, pitted and cubed
avocados, add to the dressing.
Gently add 4 cups of thinly sliced celery,
And 2 thinly sliced green onion.
Garnish with water cress.

My Photo/ 10

13

Golden Apple Salad

Core 2 unpeeled Golden Delicious apples, cut into cubes and coat with lemon juice. Drain 1 can pineapple tid bits, reserving 1 tb. of juice. Mix together apples, pineapple and 2 medium size shredded carrots. Combine 1 3 oz. room temperature cream cheese with the saved juice, add 1 1/2 tsp. grated lemon peel, 2 tsp. sugar, 1/4 tsp. ground nutmeg and salt, blend well, gently mix with apple mixture. Mound apple mixture on greens and sprinkle with salted chopped nuts.

Nic's Photo/06

Chef's Salad

Tare and washed head lettuce into bite size pieces. Toss with a French Dressing mixed with a pinch of oregano. Add 1 tomato cut in quarters and toss again. Garnish with 1/2 cup diced Swiss Cheese, 1/2 diced cucumber, 1/2 thinly sliced bell pepper

Yogurt Rice

Cook 2 cups brown rice in 1 tsp. salt, 4 cups water for 45 minutes. Chop 1/2 green pepper fine. Add to rice with 2 tb. finely minced fresh ginger and 2 cups yogurt. Cool for a few hours as to marinate before serving.

Green Shades Salad

Wash and dry 1 head leaf lettuce, 1/2 bunch spinach, 1/2 cup green peas, 1/4 cup toasted sunflower seeds, chop 1/2 cup green pepper. Add 1/4 cup Green Goddess Dressing and toss.

Dressing...

Mix together 1 cup mayo. 1 avocado peeled and pitted, 2 tb. chopped green onion, 1 tb. lemon juice, 1 clove chopped garlic, salt and pepper to taste.

15

Garry's Photos

Potato Salad

Peel 4 to 5 potatoes, cut in quarters and boil until tender, refrigerate until cooled. Boil 4 to 5 eggs until hard, cool with potatoes. After cooling chop potatoes and eggs in a large bowl. Chop 1/2 onion, 1 stalk of celery, salt and pepper to taste, add to potato mixture. Mix in 1 tsp. mustard and just enough mayonnaise to moisten. Sprinkle with paprika.

My Photos

16

Western Potato Pie

Preheat oven at 350. Heat a nonstick skillet with 1 1/2 tb. oil, add 1 cup pared cooked diced potatoes, 1/2 cup diced green pepper, 1/2 cup diced onion, saute over medium heat, frequently stir until lightly browned. Spray a 9 inch pie plate with oil. Spread potato mixture in bottom of pie plate. In a bowl beat 4 eggs, 3/4 cup buttermilk, 1/4 tsp.salt and pepper, pour over potato mixture and sprinkle with grated swiss cheese. Arrange 1 sliced tomato overlapping slices, sprinkle with grated Parmesan cheese. Bake 35 to 40 minutes or until lightly browned and cooked through. Remove from oven and let stand for 10 minutes before slicing.

Sour Cream Potato Casserole

Saute 1/2 cup finely chopped onion in 2 tb. butter until soft.

Slice 5 large cooked potatoes into a buttered casserole dish.

Sprinkle the cooked onions, 1/4 cup dry bread crumbs and

1/4 cup grated cheddar cheese evenly over potatoes.

In a bowl beat 2 eggs and 1 cup sour cream with salt and

pepper. Pour over potatoes, sprinkle with another 1/4 cup

cheddar cheese, bake at 350 until golden brown and tender.

18

My Photo/08

Scalloped Cabbage

Wash and slice 4 cups of cabbage. Cook in a small amount of salted water in a covered saucepan until tender and drain. Use a buttered casserole dish with 1/3 cup chopped canned tomatoes with 1 cup white sauce. Sprinkle with 1/2 cup bread crumbs and 1/2 cups grated cheddar cheese down into the cabbage mixture, bake in a 350 oven for 25 minutes or until browned.

For the white sauce melt 2 tb. margarine in a saucepan, stir in 1/2 tsp salt, 1/8 tsp. pepper and stir in a little at a time 2 tb. flour until well blended. Add 1 cup milk slowly, cook and stir continually over medium heat until boiling and cooked to desired thickness. Remove from heat and pour over recipe.

Italian Style Broccoli

Wash and trim stalks and remove large leaves. Cut stalks and flowerets into large pieces. Heat 1/4 cup oil in a large skillet. Add 1 peeled and mashed clove of garlic, 1/3 cleaned and minced onion and 1/4 tsp. chilli powder. Stir and heat until onion is soft, remove garlic and discard. Add 1 1/2 lb. broccoli, 2 tb. water and 1 tsp salt. Cover and cook 12 to 15 minutes or until tender, serve immediately.

20

My Photo

Country Style Eggplant

Preheat oven at 350. Saute 1 medium pared and cubed eggplant for 5 minutes, in 3 tb. butter in a large skillet. Pour into greased casserole dish. In the skillet saute 1/2 cup diced onion for 2 minutes, stir in 1 can chopped tomatoes, add 1 tb. finely chopped parsley, 1 tsp. sugar, 1/2 tsp. chilli powder, 1 tsp. salt and 1/8 tsp. pepper. Stir until it comes to a boil. Pour over eggplant. Sprinkle with 1 cup bread crumbs and 1/2 cup grated cheese. Bake for 45 minutes or until browned and bubbly. 6 servings.

21

My Photo/09

Eggplant Parmesan

Preheat oven at 350. Wash and cut eggplant in thick slices. Dip each slice into 3 beaten eggs, then into 1 cup dry bread crumbs. In a skillet saute in hot oil until golden brown on both sides. Place browned eggplant layered in a greased casserole dish. Sprinkle 1/2 cup grated Parmesan cheese, 2 tsp. oregano, 1/2 lb. sliced Mozzarella cheese. Cover with 1 8 oz. can of tomato sauce. Repeat layers until all eggplant is used up, topping last layer with sauce then Mozzarella. Bake, uncovered for 30 minutes or until cheese has melted. 4 to 6 servings.

Garry's Photo/09

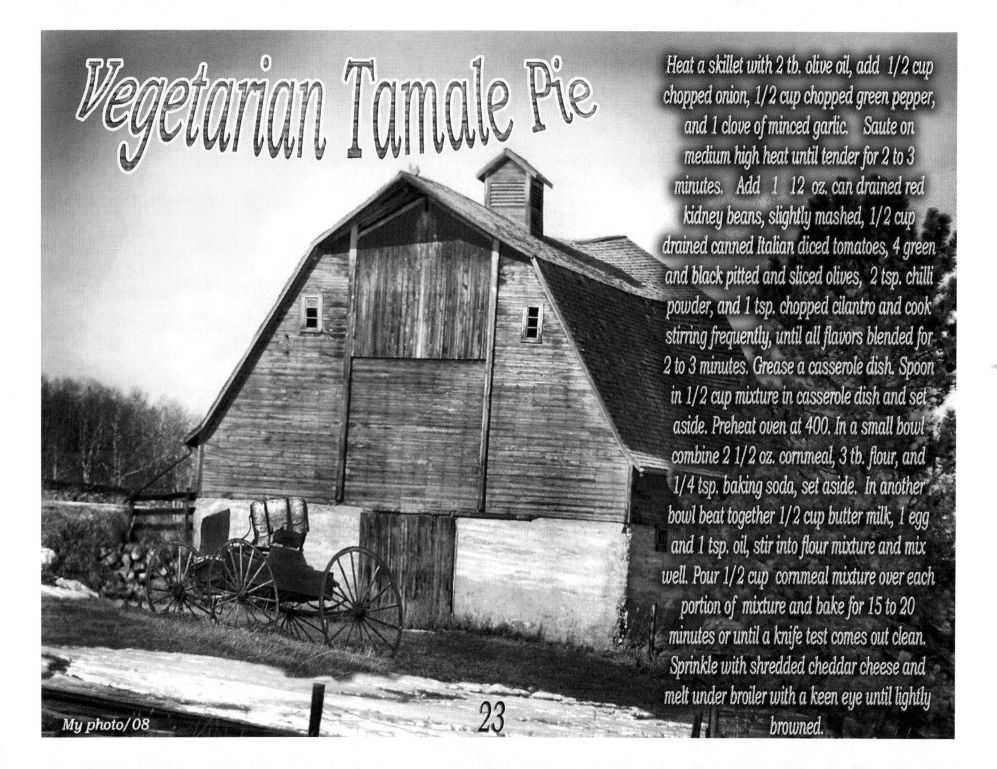

Vegetarian Tamale Pie

Heat a skillet with 2 tb. olive oil, add 1/2 cup chopped onion, 1/2 cup chopped green pepper, and 1 clove of minced garlic. Saute on medium high heat until tender for 2 to 3 minutes. Add 1 12 oz. can drained red kidney beans, slightly mashed, 1/2 cup drained canned Italian diced tomatoes, 4 green and black pitted and sliced olives, 2 tsp. chilli powder, and 1 tsp. chopped cilantro and cook stirring frequently, until all flavors blended for 2 to 3 minutes. Grease a casserole dish. Spoon in 1/2 cup mixture in casserole dish and set aside. Preheat oven at 400. In a small bowl combine 2 1/2 oz. cornmeal, 3 tb. flour, and 1/4 tsp. baking soda, set aside. In another bowl beat together 1/2 cup butter milk, 1 egg and 1 tsp. oil, stir into flour mixture and mix well. Pour 1/2 cup cornmeal mixture over each portion of mixture and bake for 15 to 20 minutes or until a knife test comes out clean. Sprinkle with shredded cheddar cheese and melt under broiler with a keen eye until lightly browned.

My photo/ 08

23

Cheesie Corn Casserole

Preheat oven at 350. Prepare 2 12 oz. pkg. frozen kernel corn, cut and core 1 green pepper, cut off 3 rings and chop the rest of the pepper. In a sauce pan heat 1/4 cup butter, stir in the chopped green pepper, add 1 small finely chopped onion, cook until onion is transparent, remove and set aside. Blend in the sauce pan, 2 tb. butter if needed, add 2 tb. flour with 1/2 tsp. salt, 1/4 tsp. dry mustard and a pinch of pepper, gradually stir to mix and blend smooth. Gradually add 1 1/2 cup milk, cook stirring constantly until thickened. Remove from heat and stir in corn and onion mixture. Turn into a greased casserole dish. In another bowl beat 1 egg then add 1 1/2 cup broken into small pieces of cheese twist into corn mixture, mix evenly. sprinkle 1/2 cup crushed cheese twist, Bake for 25 to 30 minutes, Garnish with pepper rings.

My Photo

Cauliflower A LA Huntington

As a head of cauliflower has been cleaned and broken into pieces and is cooking. Mix together to make a sauce in a double boiler starting with 1 1/2 tsp. mustard, 1 1/4 tsp. salt, 1 tsp. sugar, 1/4 tsp. paprika, 1/4 cup salad oil, 3 slightly beaten egg yolks, mix well. Then mix in 1/2 cup vinegar, 1/2 tsp. onion flakes, 1/2 tsp. curry powder, 2 tsp. butter and 1 tsp. finely chopped parsley. Stir until thickened. Pour over the cooked and drained cauliflower, serve hot.

Garry's Photo

Herbed Fluffy Potatoes

Preheat oven at 350   Prepare 3 cups mashed potatoes. Combine 1 8 oz. container French onion chip dip, 1 cup cream style cottage cheese, 2 egg yolks, 1 tb. finely chopped green onion 1 tb. dried parsley flakes, pinch nutmeg and a pinch of pepper. Beat 2 egg whites until stiff but moist peaks, fold into potato mixture. Turn into a greased casserole dish and dot with 1 tb. margarine. Bake for 55 to 60 minutes or until set or set under broiler until lightly browned.

My Photo/08

Aggie's Cream Peas

In a sauce pan add 3 tb. margarine and melt on medium heat add 1/4 cup finely chopped onion and cook just until transparent add 2 tb. flour a little at a time until blended smooth. Pour in 1 can of peas with liquid, stir until thickened, serve hot.

My Photo/ 09

Ratatouille

Means vegetable soup or stew in French

Chop 1 large onion coarsely, cut 1 green pepper into squares, slice zucchini into 1/2 inch rounds, dice egg plant into 1 inch cubes, In a heavy sauce pan, saute the onion, 1/2 clove minced garlic and green pepper in 1/4 cup olive oil until soft, stir in eggplant and zucchini and saute a few more minutes. Add 3 chopped tomatoes and season with 1 tsp. salt, 1/8 tsp.pepper, 1/2 tsp. basil, 1/2 tsp. oregano, cover and simmer on low heat for 30 minutes or until vegetables are cooked. Uncover and turn heat up to cook off some of the liquid.

28

Cindy's Photo/07

Fast & Easy Vegetable Soup

In a sauce pan saute 1 tb. margarine with 1 cup chopped onion until soft. Add 2 cups grated carrots, 2 cups chopped cabbage and 1/2 cup of rice, brown slightly, add 2 tsp. salt and 8 cups boiling water, cover and simmer slowly for 1 hour. Add 1 19 fl. oz. canned tomatoes or tomato juice, add water if needed.

My Photos/09

Gulyassuppe

In a large pot saute 2 medium chopped onions in 2 tb. oil until transparent. Add 1 lb. cubed chuck steak, and brown slightly. Add 1 tb. paprika, 1/2 tsp. caraway seeds, 1/4 tsp. marjoram and 1 clove, crushed garlic, cook for 1 minute. Add 6 cups water, 2 tb. beef bouillon base, 1 tsp. salt, 3 tomatoes cubed, 3 potatoes peeled and cubed. Bring to a boil, drop the heat and simmer for 45 minutes. Serve hot with crusty rolls.

cream of Pea Soup

In a sauce pan add 2 tb. butter add 1/4 cup chopped onion, 1 clove crushed garlic, cook until soft, about 3 minutes. Add 1 tb. flour and blend well. Add 2 cups chicken broth, bring to a boil stirring constantly. Add 3 cups frozen peas and heat for 5 minutes, puree in blender and return to heat and stir in 1/2 cup whipped cream, add salt if needed.

My Photo/09

31

Borsch

In a large sauce pan add 2 tb. butter over medium heat. Add 1/2 cup of chopped onions and cook for 4 to 5 minutes until just soft, not browned. Add 5 cups peeled and chopped beets, 1/4 cup red wine vinegar, 1 tsp. sugar, 1 tsp. salt, and pepper to taste. Add 1/2 cup beef stock and simmer, covered for 45 minutes. Then add 1 3/4 qt. of beef stock, and add 4 sprigs of parsley and 1 bay leaf tied and simmer for another 30 minutes. Sprinkle with 1/2 cup finely chopped dill. Serve hot with a dollop of sour cream.

Cindy's Photo /07

Watercress Soup

Chop 2 bunches watercress. In a large kettle, saute 2 onions diced in 4 tb. butter, add 1 large diced potato, watercress and 6 cups chicken broth, season with salt and pepper. Cover and simmer on medium heat until potatoes are tender. Puree batches in blender and reheat in soup pot and add 2 cups of light cream, mix well.

My Photos

33

Cream Of Celery Soup

Cut 3 cups celery into small pieces and cook in 2 cups water until soft. In a small sauce pan make a white sauce using 1 tb. butter melted in a double boiler, add 2 slices of chopped onion. Cook until transparent then add 1 tb. flour adding a little at a time until blended smoothly. Slowly add 3 cups milk stirring to blend evenly on medium heat until thickened, add celery and the water stirring constantly to evenly blend. Season with 1 tb. chicken broth, mix with salt and pepper.

Serve Hot.

To prevent boil overs add a lump of butter or cooking oil.

Cindy's Photo/07

Cream Of Carrot Soup

Cook 1 medium chopped onion in 2 tb. butter for 5 minutes until soft, add 1/2 cup fine bread crumbs, 1 cup milk, 1 tsp. salt and 1/8 tsp. pepper. Stir to blend in 4 cups vegetable stock and 1 tb. sugar.

Add 2 cups shredded carrots Simmer for 20 minutes. Serve hot.

35

My Photo/08

Cheesy Easy Beer Soup

Simmer 2 to 3 egg shells in your home made soup stock helps to clarify the broth.

In a sauce pan, mix 2 cans cream of chicken soup and season with 1 tsp. Worcestershire sauce, 1/4 tsp. pepper, 1/4 tsp. paprika, add 2 cans beer gradually while stirring, heat to a simmer. Add 2 cups shredded cheddar cheese, stirring constantly until cheese has melted. Serve hot.

My photo/09

Muffins & Quick Breads

Yeast Breads

PIONEER OLDS

My Photo/08

Refrigerator Bran Muffins

In a large bowl, combine 4 cups whole wheat flour, 3 cups bran, 3/4 cup brown sugar, 1 tsp. salt, 2 tsp. baking soda and 1 cup raisins. In a medium bowl, beat 4 eggs, beat in 3/4 cup vegetable oil, 1 1/2 cups molasses and and 2 1/2 cups buttermilk. Pour into bran mixture, blend gently but thoroughly. Cover and refrigerate 24 hours before using, can store in refrigerator up to 3 weeks and makes 5 dozen muffins. To Bake. Set oven at 350 and fill a greased muffin tin 3/4 full and bake for 30 to 40 minutes, test with a tooth pick for doneness

My Photo/09

Master Mix

Sift 9 cups flour, 1/3 cup baking powder, 1 tb. salt, 1 tb. cream of tarter and 1/4 cup sugar. Sift all dry ingredients 3 times. Cut in 2 cups of margarine until mix resembles corn meal. Store in refrigerator in a covered container. To measure pile into a cup and level. This recipe has been put together to cut down on baking time. Great for dumplings and biscuits or add eggs, sugar, spices and fruit for muffins to coffee cakes if you follow with the main ingredients and half the work has been done. Just add to create.

39

My Photo/Graphics

Rhubarb Muffins

Combine 2 1/2 cups flour, 1 tsp. baking powder, 1 tsp. baking soda, 1/2 tsp. salt. In another bowl combine 1 1/4 cup packed brown sugar, 1/2 cup oil, 1 beaten egg, and 2 tsp. vanilla, stir in 1 1/2 cups diced rhubarb and 1 cup butter milk, mix to combine, add to dry mixture, mix just until moist though. Spoon into a greased muffin tin 3/4 full. Sprinkle with topping of 1/2 cup sugar, 1 1/2 tsp. cinnamon, mix in 1 tb. butter. Bake in a 400 oven, for 20 minutes or until a tooth pick comes out clean.

Carrot Pineapple Muffins

In a bowl combine 1 1/2 cups flour, 1 cup sugar, 1 tsp. baking powder, 1 tsp. baking soda, 1/2 tsp. salt, and 1/2 tsp. cinnamon. In another bowl mix together 2 eggs, 1 cup grated carrots, 2/3 cup oil, 1/2 cup drained crushed pineapple and 1 tsp. vanilla mix well. Add to dry ingredients just to moisten. Fill a greased muffin tin 3/4 full. Bake in a 350 oven for 25 minutes or until done.

My Photo/09

Mexican Muffins

Preheat oven at 400. Mix 1 1/2 cups of the Master mix in a bowl with 1/2 cup yellow cornmeal, 1/2 cup cream style corn, 1 tb. sugar, 2 tb. milk, 1/4 tsp. chili powder, 1 4 oz. can whole green chilies, drained, seeded, and chopped, 1 2 oz. jar drained, diced pimientos and 1 egg. Beat vigorously for 30 seconds. Fill batter in a well greased muffin tin 2/3 full bake 20 to 25 minutes or until golden brown.

41

My Photos/09

Old Fashion Cornmeal Muffins

Mix together 1/3 cup flour, 3 tb. sugar, 1 tsp. baking powder, 1/2 tsp. soda and 1/2 tsp. salt. Stir in 1 cup cornmeal. Combine 1 1/2 cups sour cream, 1 beaten egg and 2 tb. melted butter. Add to the dry ingredients, stir just to blend. Fill batter in a well greased muffin tin 3/4 full. Bake in a 400 oven for 25 to 30 minutes.

42

My Photo/09

Spooned Bread Spud Muffins

Heat 3/4 cup water, add 1 tb. butter and 1/2 tsp. salt to a boil, stir in enough instant mashed potatoes for 2 servings. Mix together well. Add 2 eggs 1 at a time, beating after each addition, beat in 3/4 cup milk. In another bowl mix together 1 cup cornmeal, 1 tsp. baking powder, 1/2 tsp. salt, stir into potato mixture, fold in 1/4 cup crumbled bacon bits. Spoon into a well greased muffin tin 3/4 inch full. Sprinkle tops with bacon bits. Bake in a 350 oven for 20 to 25 minutes or until golden in color.

Garrys Photo/08

43

Sour Cream Gems

2 egg yolks is equal to 1 egg. A little vinegar added to the water when boiling a cracked egg will prevent the white from boiling out.

In a bowl beat 2 eggs with 1/4 cup sugar, mix in 1 cup of sour cream, stir in 2 cups master mix , 1/2 tsp. nutmeg, 1/2 tsp. grated lemon peel, just until moistened. Fold in 2/3 cup seedless golden raisins. Fill in a greased muffin tin evenly. Bake in a 375 oven for 15 to 20 minutes or until a tooth pick comes out clean.

44

My Photo/ 06

Buttermilk Biscuits

Combine 2 cups sifted flour, 1/2 tsp. salt, 1/2 tsp. soda, 3 tsp. baking powder in a mixing bowl, cut in 2 tb. margarine until the texture of cornmeal. Add 1 cup buttermilk, stirring a little at a time until mixed evenly. Turn onto a floured board, knead gently several times until it forms into a ball. Pat out to 1/4 inch thick. Cut into rounds with a floured biscuit cutter. Place on a well greased baking sheet 1/2 inch apart. Bake in a 400 oven for 12 to 15 minutes. Serve hot.

My Photo/07

English Scones

Preheat oven to 450. Combine 2 cups flour, 2 tb. sugar, 1 tb. baking powder, 1/2 tsp. salt. Cut in 1/4 cup shorting with a pastry cutter until the size of peas, add 1/2 cups currants. In a separate bowl, beat eggs until light, reserve some egg to brush the tops of scones. Stir in 1/2 cup milk. Make a well in the center of dry ingredients. Add liquids all at once, stirring vigorously with a fork until it comes from the sides of bowl. Turn onto a floured board, pat dough to 3/4 inch thickness. Cut into triangles, brush with egg wash. Sprinkle with sugar.

Bake on a ungreased baking sheet for 12 to 15 minutes.

Crumpets

In a large bowl add 1/2 cup warm water and 2 tsp. sugar, stir until dissolved, sprinkle 1 tb. yeast, set for 5 minutes or until bubbles. Add 1 1/2 cups milk, 1/2 tsp. baking soda and 1 tsp. salt. Gradually add 2 1/2 cups flour and blend well. Set in a warm place for 1/2 hour. Grease a heavy skillet with crumpet rings or cookie cutters and preheat all. Pour about 3 tb. full into each ring, cook over medium heat until set and full of bubbles formed on top, remove ring and flip to brown on the other side. Repeat until batter is used up.

Garrys Photo/09

Herbed Beer Bread

Saute 1 cup finely chopped onions in 1 tb. butter just until tender, do not brown, remove and set aside. In a large bowl combine 3 cups flour, 3 tsp. baking powder, 1/2 tsp. salt, 1 tsp. oregano and 1/4 tsp. rosemary. Add 2 tb. sugar, mix to blend evenly. Add 1 can beer and the onions, stir until all dry ingredients are moistened, do not over mix. Pour into a greased loaf pan, give the pan a hard knock on the counter a few times to even dough out evenly, brush tops with an egg wash. Let stand at room temperature for 10 minutes. Bake on the bottom rack at 375 for 50 to 60 minutes.

Garrys Photo/ 08

Welsh Cakes

Mix together as a pastry, 2 cups flour, 1 cup sugar, 2 tsp. baking powder, 1/4 tsp. nutmeg, and 1/2 tsp. cinnamon. Cut in 1/4 cup shortening until crumbly. Mix in 1 cup currants or raisins. In a bowl beat 2 eggs using a little milk to mix with eggs. Mix into dry ingredients if needed.

Roll out with rolling pin, and cut with a round cutter, Cook in a skillet with a small amount of margarine until brown, flip to brown on each side

Garrys Photos/ My Graphics/ Nics fine Graphics

French Breakfast Puffs

Preheat oven to 350. Mix together butter and shortening to make 1/3 cup. Add 1/2 cup sugar and 1 beaten egg thoroughly. Sift 1 1/2 cups flour, 1 1/2 tsp. baking powder, 1/2 tsp. salt, 1/2 tsp. nutmeg. Stir into sugar mixture alternately with 1/2 cup milk. Fill greased muffin tins 2/3 full. Bake for 20 to 25 minutes. Remove from oven, roll tops in butter then sugar and cinnamon immediately, serve hot.

My Photo/09

Cheesy Popovers

50

Mix 2 beaten eggs, 1 cup milk, 1 tb. melted shortening together. Add 1 cup sifted flour and 1/2 tsp. salt. If desired, add 1/2 cup grated cheddar cheese. Beat with a beater until smooth. Pour into a hot oiled muffin pan, filling half full. Bake in a 425 oven for 40 minutes.

My Photo/ 09

Zucchini Pineapple Loaf

Sift together 3 cups flour, 1 tsp. salt, 1 tsp. baking soda, 1/2 tsp. baking powder, 1 1/2 tsp. cinnamon and 3/4 tsp. nutmeg. Then add 1 cup chopped nuts. In another bowl beat 3 eggs, 1 3/4 cups sugar, mix in 1 cup oil, 2 tsp. vanilla, 1 3/4 cup grated unpeeled zucchini and 1 10 oz. can drained crushed pineapple. Stir dry ingredients into egg mixture evenly. Pour into 2 well greased loaf pans evenly and bake in a 350 oven for 50 to 60 minutes.

51

Garrys Photo/08

Lemon Bread

Cream 1/2 cup butter and 1 cup sugar together, mix well. Add 2 eggs, beat until creamy." Add 1/2 cup milk and 1 grated rind of lemon. In another bowl mix together 1 1/2 cups flour, 1 tsp. baking powder, 1/2 cup coconut or 1/2 cup chopped nuts, mix to blend. Combine dry ingredients into wet mixture well. Bake in a greased loaf pan in a preheated 350 oven for 45 to 50 minutes. Frost with a mixture of 1/4 cup powdered sugar and juice from 1 squeezed lemon. Spoon over loaf. Remove from pan when cooled.

My Photo/ 08

Banana Loaf

In a large bowl mix together 1 1/2 cups flour,
2 tsp. baking powder, 1/4 tsp. baking soda,
1 tsp. salt, stir in 1/2 chopped walnuts.
In another bowl cream together 1/3 cup
margarine, then mix in 2/3 cup sugar.
Add 2 beaten eggs combine well.
Mix in dry ingredients alternate with 1 cup
of mashed banana beat after each addition.
Pour into a well greased loaf pan. Set aside for
15 to 20 minutes to fill any air pockets. Bake in
a preheated oven for 50 to 55 minutes or until a
toothpick comes out clean.

53

Garry's Photo/ 10

Walnut Carrot Bread

Preheat oven to 350. Grease 4 large loaf pans. Beat 4 eggs, gradually add 1 1/2 cups brown sugar, then 3/4 cup oil. In another bowl combine 3 cups flour, 1 1/2 tsp. baking soda, 3/4 tsp. baking powder, 3/4 tsp. salt, 2 tsp cinnamon. Add to egg mixture alternately with 2 cups peeled grated carrots. Stir in 1 cup coarsely chopped walnuts and 1 tsp. vanilla. Pour evenly into loaf pans, Bake for 60 minutes, cool for 15 minutes before removing from pans.

54

My Photos/09

Fruit & Nut Bread

Sift together 2 cups flour, 4 tsp. baking powder, 1/2 tsp. salt into a mixing bowl. Add 1/2 cup sugar, 3/4 cup slivered almonds, 1/2 cup raisins, 1/2 cup chopped dates and 2 tb. orange rind. Mix well. In another bowl add 3/4 cup milk, 1/4 cup orange juice, 2 tb. melted butter to 1 beaten egg, mix to combine. Add wet ingredients to flour mixture, blend well. Pour into a greased loaf pan, let stand for 20 minutes. Preheat oven to 350 and bake for 55 to 60 minutes in the centre of the oven on middle rack. Cool for several hours on a rack before slicing.

55

My Photo/09

Butter Milk Pan Rolls

Preheat oven at 400. In a large bowl combine 1 cup flour, 1 pkg. yeast, 2 tb. sugar, 1 tsp. salt, 1/2 tsp. soda, mix well. In a sauce pan heat 1 cup butter milk, 1/4 cup water and 1/4 cup shortening until warm. Add to flour mixture. Blend at a low speed with a hand mixer until moistened then 2 minutes on medium speed. Stir in by hand gradually enough flour to make a soft dough. Turn on to floured board and knead until smooth about 2 minutes. Press dough into a greased 9 inch square pan. Sprinkle lightly with flour. Cut 12 rolls with a table knife almost to the bottom of pan. Cover and let rise in a warm place for 30 minutes. Bake for 15 to 20 minutes or until golden brown. Serve hot.

56

Kolache
koh-lotch-eh

In a large bowl, combine 1 1/2 cup flour, 1 pkg. yeast, 1/4 cup sugar, and 1 tsp. salt, mix well. In a sauce pan, heat 3/4 cup milk, 1/4 cup water and 1/4 cup margarine just until warm. Add to flour mixture, add 1 egg, blend on a low speed with a mixture to blend evenly then beat on medium for three minutes. Gradually stir in by hand the remaining flour to make a soft dough. Turn onto a floured board and knead until smooth and elastic, about 3 minutes. Place in a greased bowl, turn over to coat grease on all sides. and cover, place in a warm place until double in size. about 1 hour. Punch down dough and divide into 2 parts on a floured board, roll each part into a 12 inch square. Cut each square into 9 4 in. squares. Spoon filling in center. Brush with water to the corner, fold opposite corner over and seal. Place on a greased baking sheet and cover. Let rise in a warm place until almost double size about 20 minutes. Brush with butter. Bake in a 375 oven for 12 to 15 minutes until golden brown. Serve warm or cold.

My Photo/09

Orange Filling.......... In a small bowl blend 1 1/3 cup orange marmalade, 1/3 cup chopped nuts and 1 tsp. lemon juice. mix well. Spoon 1 tb. of filling into each Kolache. Filling for 18 kolache makes 1 1/2 cups.

Cream Cheese Raisin Filling..............In a small bowl, mix 2 pkg. 3oz. soften cream cheese,2 tb. sugar, 1 egg, 1 tsp.rind from a lemon beat until smooth and creamy. Stir in 1/4 cup chopped golden raisins. Use 2 tsp.for each, 18 kolache makes 1 cup.

Cranberry Orange Filling.....In a bowl combine 2/3 cup canned cranberry, 1/3 cup marmalade, 1/3 cup vanilla wafer crumbs, 1/4 cup chopped nuts with a dash of cinnamon, 2 tsp. for each.

Basic Refrigerator Bread or Rolls

Cream 1/2 cup sugar with 2 tb. margarine in a large mixing bowl. In another bowl combine 1/2 cup warm water with 1 tsp. sugar and 1 pkg. dry yeast, stir until dissolved. Pour 1 cup of very hot water over creamed mixture, stir until dissolved. Add 1 cup cold water and 1 beaten egg, stir to mix well, add yeast mixture, stir well.

In a large bowl add 2 tsp. salt, 4 cups flour, stir in yeast mixture well, rest for 5 minutes add 2 more cups flour and mix again. Turn onto a floured board kneading in more flour as you knead until elastic. Place in a greased bowl turn once to oil top of dough. Cover with a clean tea towel, place in to the refrigerator until needed. Form dough into loafs or shaped rolls. Palace in or on a greased pan. Let rise until double in size. Bake in a 375 oven for 20 to 25 minutes for rolls and 45 minutes for loafs or until golden brown.

58

My Photo/08

Bread Machine Carrot Bread

Add in bread machine in this order.
2 cup water, 1 cup grated carrots 3 cups flour,
1/2 tb. salt, 3 tb. sugar, 2 tb. butter and 3 tsp.
fast rising yeast. Select white bread on your
bread machine. Press start. Check after
5 minutes, add water if to dry or flour if to wet
1 tb. at a time.

Bread Machine Apple Cinnamon Bread

Add in bread machine in this order.

1/3 cup applesauce, 2 tb. margarine 1 3/4 cup
milk, 2 1/2 cups flour, 1 tsp. cinnamon, 1 tsp.
salt, 2 tb. brown sugar, 3 tsp. fast rising yeast.
Press start.

My Photo/09

Caramel Butter Buns

Heat 1 cup water to lukewarm, pour 1/2 of the cup warm water into a bowl and dissolve 1 tsp. sugar, add 1 pkg. yeast, let stand for 15 minutes. Add the remaining 1/2 cup water, add 1 tsp. salt, 1/2 cup sugar, 1/3 cup soft butter and 4 beaten eggs. Add the yeast mixture stir well. In a large bowl sift 4 1/2 cups flour, make a well in the centre. Pour the liquid into the centre of flour. Stir until liquid disappears. Mix the dough with floured hands, forming into a ball. Place into a greased bowl, spread grease on all sides of dough, cover with wax paper and a tight lid. Allow dough to rise for 2 hours. Punch down several times, remove to a greased baking sheet, roll into a cylinder shape, about 1 1/2 inch thick. With a greased knife cut into 36 pieces of uniform size, roll into balls with a floured palm of hand, press slightly Grease. 2 8x8 cake pan, place dough loosely in pan. Cover and let rise 1 hour.

Bake buns at 350 for 20 minutes or until golden brown. Cool on a rack, ice. separately when serving.

Caramel Icing

Combine 1/2 cup sugar, 2 tb. butter and 1 tb. water in a sauce pan. Boil for 10 minutes, stirring constantly. Slowly beat in 1/2 cup icing sugar. Thin to the right consistency with 3 tb. of cream. Ice buns Immediately.

My Photo/ 08

Italian Bread Sticks

In medium bowl dissolve 1 pkg. yeast and 1 tsp. sugar in 2/3 cup warm water. Add 2 tb. olive oil, 1 tsp. salt and 1 cup flour; mix in well. Add 1 1/4 cups more flour to make a stiff dough. Turn out on a floured board and knead until smooth and elastic, about 5 minutes adding more flour as needed. Place dough in a greased bowl, use hands to grease dough on all sides. Cover with a damp towel and let rise in a warm place until double size. Punch down and divide in half, cut each half into 24 equal size pieces, roll each using palms of hands into 6 to 8 inches in lengths. Place on a greased baking sheet about 1/2 inch apart. Brush with 1 beaten egg and sprinkle with sesame seeds. Let rise in a warm place until double size, about 30 minutes. Bake in a 325 oven for 30 minutes or until golden.

61

My Photo/07

Grandma's Dinner Rolls

In a large bowl combine 1 1/2 cups flour 2 tsp. sugar 1 tsp. salt and 1 pkg. quick active yeast. Add 1 cup warm water, 2 tb. vegetable oil and 1 beaten egg. Mix with a wooden spoon, stir in 1 cup flour beaten until smooth scraping batter down into bowl. Cover and let rise until double size. Place in a greased muffin pan, let rise again until twice the twice the size. Bake at 400 until golden brown about 25 to 30 minutes.

Currant Buns
Krentenbollen

Dissolve 1 pkg. fast rise yeast in 1 1/2 cup warm milk. and 1 tb. sugar in a large bowl. Add a pinch of salt, and 1 slightly beaten egg stir to mix, Add 3 cup flour, alternating with 1/2 cup currants, 1/4 cup raisons, 1/4 cup finely chopped candied fruit. and 1/4 cup chopped walnuts. Shape into balls. Place on a greased baking sheet 1 inch apart. Cover and let rise for 1 hour. Bake in a preheated oven at 400 for 20 minutes or until lightly browned, butter

My Photo/ 08

Herb Casserole Bread

Soften 1 pkg. dry yeast in 1/4 cup warm water. Heat 3/4 cup milk until warm. Add 1 1/2 4 oz. pkg. crumbled blue cheese, 1 tb. finely chopped onion and 1 tb. butter. Mix to blend. Turn into a large bowl, add 1 tb. sugar, 1/2 tsp salt, 1 tb. dill weed, 2 tsp. chopped dried parsley and 1 cup flour. Beat to blend, add 1 1/4 cup more flour, blend in thoroughly. Cover and let rise in a warm place until it is double size, about 45 minutes. Stir down and place in a well greased casserole dish. Let rise again in warm place until double rise, approximately 30 minutes. Bake in a 350 oven for 35 to 40 minutes, cool to slice.

63

My Photo/09

Coffee Can Bread

Dissolve 1 pkg dry yeast in 1/2 cup water in large mixing bowl, Blend in 1/8 tsp. ginger. 1/3 cup sugar, let stand in warm place until bubbly, about 15 minutes.

Stir in 1/4 cup sugar, 3/4 cup milk, 1 tsp. salt, 2 tb. vegetable oil. Gradually add 4 to 5 cups flour, mixing 1 to 2 cups with a wooden spoon until unable to beat it in easily. Knead dough using as much of the left over flour as possible to knead in.. Place dough in a 2 lb. well greased coffee can. Cover with a well greased plastic can lid, let rise in warm place until lid pops off. Bake in a 350 oven for 50 to 60 minutes. Cool on rack for 10 minutes, bang hard to loosen. edges, use knife to slide out.

64

Coffee Cakes

Cakes

Lades Tea Party

My Photo/09

Overnight Coffee Cake

Cream 2/3 cup shortening or margarine with 1/2 cup brown sugar, 1 cup white sugar, add 2 eggs, mix just to blend. In a large bowl combine 2 cups flour, 1 tsp. baking powder, 1/2 tsp salt, 1 tsp. cinnamon. Add to egg mixture alternating with 1 cup buttermilk using a electric mixer on low just until moistened continue for 3 minutes. If you don't have buttermilk you could add 1 tb. vinegar to 1 cup milk to sour it." Pour batter into greased and floured 9 x 13 pan. Cover with topping.

Top with a mixture of 1/2 cup brown sugar, 1 tsp. cinnamon, 1/2 tsp. nutmeg, 1/2 cup chopped walnuts. Combine and cover cake and refrigerate overnight. Remove and put directly into a 350 oven for 30 to 40 minutes.

Party Coffee Cake

Cream 1 cup butter and 1 cup sugar well, add 1 cup corn syrup. Add 4 eggs 1 at a time and beat well. Pour in 1 cup cold liquid coffee, 1 tsp. baking soda, 1 1/2 tsp. cloves, 1 tsp. cinnamon. Blend in 4 cups flour gradually, stir to blend evenly. Pour into 1 large greased baking pan or 2 smaller pans. Bake in a 350 oven for 60 minutes.

66

Garry's Photo/08

Crumb Cake

With hands rub together to make a crumb mixture 3/4 cup margarine, 1 cup sugar, 2 cups flour, 2 tsp. baking powder, 1/2 tsp. cloves, 1 tsp. cinnamon, 1/4 tsp. salt. Save 1/3 cup crumb mixture for topping. Add 1 well beaten egg, 1 cup buttermilk, 1/2 tsp. baking soda together then add 1/2 tsp. vanilla to crumb mixture. Pour into a greased and floured 9x9 pan and sprinkle with remaining crumb mixture. Bake in 350 oven for 35 to 40 minutes.

Garry's Photo/09

67

Cake History

People began making cakes shortly after they discovered flour. In the middle of the 18th Century yeast was no longer used for a raising agent for cakes. "They favored using the beaten eggs, beaten in as much air as possible then adding to the flour and sugar mixture to make cakes." The mixture would be then poured into molds, some very elaborate and some as simple as " two tin hoops baked on a baking sheet." Our modern cake pans developed over the years." Cakes were only for the well off. Early American cooks in each region had there own favorites. By the 1900s baking ingredients became more available with mass production and distribution on the rail roads at this time baking powder and baking soda were invented.

Baking powder consists of a combination of baking soda, cream of tarter and a moisture absorber cornstarch. It will act like yeast but much more quickly. baking powder acts immediately when adding water. There were many studies on the invention of baking powder from 1843 to 1924. In the end double acting baking powder was invented. Leaving us with today baking powder.

Garry's Photo

History Notes on Sugar

Sugar cane originally came from Asia and India. People chewed the cane raw to extract its sweetness. Indians discovered how to crystallize sugar as far back as the beginning of the Christian era.

Sugar first became known to the people of England in the 11th century. Sugar was then refined in Arabia. Crusaders brought back samples and the Arabian word sugar.

'Sugar had become an important commodity of international trade by the year 1500. A German professor in the year 1747 discovered that sugar in beet root and carrots is the same as in the sugar cane.

In 1836 farmers attempted to grow sugar beets attempted in the United States.

A series of failures made the processing of sugar beets very slow. Eventually, many plants closed because of an inability to produce good sugar.

It was finally achieved in 1877 with the operation of adequate machinery and better techniques.

By the end of the century there were 30 factories in the Western United States.

The sugar beet first appeared in Canada in 1902 in Wallaceburg Ontario, followed by in Alberta in 1903. Canada now has plants in Alberta, Manitoba and Quebec. Alberta is the chief producer with two plants.

69

My Photo/07

Hattie Spice Cake

Cream 1/2 cup butter with 2 cups sugar. Add 3 eggs 1 at a time. In another bowl combine 2 cups flour, 3 tsp. baking powder, 1/2 tsp. cloves, 1/2 tsp. cinnamon, 1/2 tsp. ginger. Add 1 cup cream and flour mixture alternately to butter mixture, fold in 2/3 cup raisins and 1/2 cup chopped walnuts and another 1/2 cup flour. Bake in a shallow well greased pan at 350 for 60 minutes.

Caramel Icing

Combine one cup brown sugar, 3 tb. butter, 3 tb. cream, boil 3 minutes and beat 3 minutes, spread on cake.

My Crow

Garry's Photo

70

Early Canadian Spiced Pumpkin Cake

Cream 1 cup shortening and 3 cups sugar. Add 3 beaten eggs, 1 can pumpkin, 1/2 tsp. vanilla, 1/2 tsp. coconut flavoring and 1 tsp. butter flavoring. In a bowl sift 3 cups flour, 1 tsp. baking soda, 1/4 tsp. salt, 1 tsp. nutmeg, 1 tsp. allspice, 1 tsp. cloves, 1 tsp. cinnamon. Add with 1 cup chopped nuts. and cream mixture. Pour into a greased and floured tube pan. Bake in a 350 oven for 1 hour and 15 minutes.

Combine 1 cup brown sugar with 1/2 cup sour cream. Cook over medium heat until sugar dissolves. Bring to a boil, simmer for 1 minute. Cool for 5 minutes. Drizzle on top of cake.

My Photo

Tomato Soup Crumb Cake

Mix 2 cups flour with 1 cup sugar together, then add 2/3 cup butter, rub with hands until crumbly, reserve 1 cup for topping. Add 1 tsp. baking soda, 1 tsp. cinnamon and 1 tsp. cloves to 1 10 oz. can tomato soup, then add to crumb mixture.

Add 1 beaten egg with 1 cup raisins and 1 cup chopped nuts. Turn into a well greased pan, sprinkle with reserved crumbs on top. Bake in a 350 oven for 40 to 50 minutes, cool in pan before cutting.

72

My Photo

Tumbler Cake

Cream 1 tumbler butter with 2 tumblers brown sugar, 1 tumbler of molasses together. Sift 5 tumblers of flour with 2 tsp. baking soda, 1 tsp. each of cloves, cinnamon and nutmeg. Dredge 3 pkg. currants, 1 lb. cut citron, 1/2 lb. lemon and orange peel, 2 lb. dates cut in pieces with a little of the dry mixture, then in the creamed mixture. Then add the remaining dry mixture, alternately with 1 tumbler of milk. Stir in 1 tumbler of strawberry jam preserves and 1/2 tumbler of good rum. Mix thoroughly and turn into 3 large bread pans filling 1 inch from the top, bake in a 250 oven for 2 hours.

Garry's Photo/09

73

Angel Cake

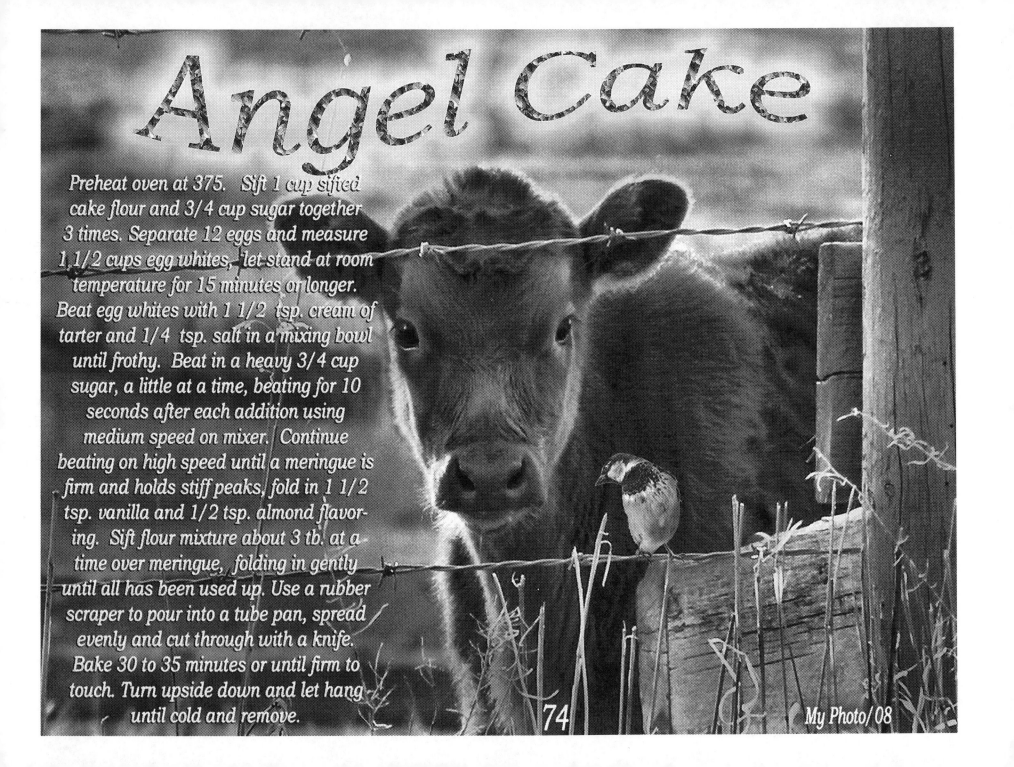

Preheat oven at 375. Sift 1 cup sifted cake flour and 3/4 cup sugar together 3 times. Separate 12 eggs and measure 1 1/2 cups egg whites, let stand at room temperature for 15 minutes or longer. Beat egg whites with 1 1/2 tsp. cream of tarter and 1/4 tsp. salt in a mixing bowl until frothy. Beat in a heavy 3/4 cup sugar, a little at a time, beating for 10 seconds after each addition using medium speed on mixer. Continue beating on high speed until a meringue is firm and holds stiff peaks, fold in 1 1/2 tsp. vanilla and 1/2 tsp. almond flavoring. Sift flour mixture about 3 tb. at a time over meringue, folding in gently until all has been used up. Use a rubber scraper to pour into a tube pan, spread evenly and cut through with a knife. Bake 30 to 35 minutes or until firm to touch. Turn upside down and let hang until cold and remove.

74

My Photo/ 08

Bride's Cake

Preheat oven at 350. Grease 2 round 10 inch layer cake pans, line with wax paper and grease. Cream 3/4 cup shortening and 2 cups sugar thoroughly, add 1 tsp. vanilla. In another bowl sift 3 cups flour, 1/2 tsp salt and 4 tsp. baking powder together. Add 1 cup milk alternately to shortening. In another bowl whip 6 egg whites, fold into batter. Add 1/2 cup chopped almonds and 1/4 cup chopped mixed candied fruit, pour into prepared pans. Bake 30 minutes or until toothpick test comes out clean. Cool in pans, then turn out on rack

Bride's Cake Frosting

Cook 2 cups sugar, 1/2 cup water and 1/8 tsp. cream of tarter in a saucepan to a soft-ball stage, add 1/8 tsp. salt to 2 egg whites in upper part of double boiler. Beat until frothy. Place over hot water and gradually add the sugar mixture, beating constantly until peaks form. Add 1 tsp. vanilla. Cover cake and decorate .

75

Heavenly Vino Cake

Sift together 2 cups flour, 2 1/2 tb. cornstarch, 1 1/2 cup sugar, 1 tb. baking powder, 1 tsp. cinnamon, 1/2 tsp. nutmeg, 1/4 tsp. allspice, 1/4 tsp. ground cloves and 1 tsp. salt in a large bowl. Mix in 3/4 cup Soave Wine, 1/2 cup vegetable oil, 1 tb. dark molasses and 1 1/2 tsp. vanilla. Beat on medium speed for 2 minutes. Mix in 1/4 cup milk and 2 eggs beat 2 more minutes. Pour into 2 greased and floured 9 inch round cake pans. Bake in a preheated 350 oven for 25 minutes, or until cake springs bake when poked. Cool 10 minutes before removing to a cooling rack.

Almond Frosting.....Beat 1 pkg. 3 oz. softened pkg. cream cheese, 1/4 cup softened butter until light and fluffy. Beat in 1 box powdered sugar, 3 tb. milk and 1 cup finely ground sugar.

76

Birthday Cake

Preheat oven at 350. Grease a 6 to 7 inch cake pan and dust with flour. Cream 1/2 cup butter, 1/2 cup brown sugar and 3 tb. golden syrup thoroughly. Add 2 beaten eggs. Sift together 1 cup flour, 1/8 tsp. salt, 1 tsp. baking powder, 1 tsp. ground mixed spice. Then add 1 1/4 cup mixed fruit such as currants, glazed cherries, and raisins. Add to creamed mixture alternately with 1 cup milk, beating well after each addition mix to a fairly soft consistency.

Place into cake pan. Bake for 1/2 hour at 350. Drop heat to 300 and bake for 2 more hours or until done.

77

Nic's Photo/07

Chocolate Potato Cake

In a large bowl mix together 3/4 cup unsweetened cocoa powder, 2 cups flour, 1 tsp. baking powder, 1 tsp. baking soda, 1/2 tsp. salt, 1 tsp. ground cinnamon, and 1 tsp. powdered instant coffee. "Set aside." In another large bowl cream together 1 cup of room temperature butter, 2 cups sugar until light and fluffy. Beat in 4 large eggs, 1 at a time. Then add 1 tsp. vanilla and 1 cup unseasoned cooled mashed potato. Beat together on low speed until smooth." On low speed blend in flour mixture alternating with 1 cup butter milk just until blended." Pour into 2 greased and floured 9 inch round baking pans. Bake in a preheated oven at 350 for 30 minutes or until tester comes out clean.

Frosting....... 3 cups powdered sugar, 1/4 cup unsweetened cocoa powder, 1/8 tsp. salt, 1/2 cup room temperature butter, 1/4 cup sour cream, 1 tsp. vanilla and 1 tb. grated orange zest. Blend until smooth, spread on cooled cake layers, top and sides.

My Photo/09

Praline Cake

Sift 2 cups flour with 2 1/2 tsp. baking powder, 1 tsp. salt and 1 1/2 cups sugar. Cream 1/2 cup shortening, sift in flour mixture, add 1 cup milk and beat in well. Add 2 eggs and 1 tsp. vanilla, beat until fluffy. Pour into a greased 13x9x2 inch baking pan. Bake in a 375 oven for 35 minutes.

Topping

Combine 1/2 cup brown sugar, 3 tb. melted butter, 2 tb. cake flour, 2 tb. water and 1 cup chopped pecans. Spread carefully over hot cake. Return to oven, bake for 5 minutes longer.

79

Princess Iced Cakes

Preheat oven at 350. Grease and flour a 9x12 inch cake pan, knock out excess flour. Cream 4 tb. butter, 4 tb. shortening together until light and fluffy. Beat in 1 cup sugar until smooth. Add 1/2 tsp. vanilla. In another bowl sift together 2 cups cake flour, 1/4 tsp. salt, 3 tsp. baking powder. Add to sugar mixture alternately with 3/4 cup milk, beating after each addition.

Whip 3/4 cup egg whites with 1/4 cup sugar until soft peaks form, fold into batter, Pour into cake pan and bake for 40 minutes, cool slightly before removing from pan onto a rack. When cooled cut into small shapes, such as rounds, squares and triangles. Frost and decorate with silver candies, coconut, or colored frosting.

My Photo/09

Honey Orange Cupcakes

Preheat oven at 350, grease 18 2 1/2 inch muffin cups. Sift 1 1/2 cups sifted cake flour, 3/4 tsp. baking soda and 3/4 tsp. salt together. Cream together 5 1/2 tb. butter or margarine, 1/2 cup strained honey, 1/4 cup sugar, 2 tsp.grated orange peel and vanilla thoroughly, add 2 eggs . Beat until light and fluffy in a mixing bowl. Add dry ingredients and 3 tb. cider vinegar alternately, beating and ending with the dry ingredients,pour into muffing tins. Bake for 20 minutes. Frost and decorate when cooled

My Photo/09

English Icebox Toffee

Grind 2/3 lb. vanilla wafers and 1 cup walnuts together. Melt 1 1/2 squares chocolate over hot water. Cream 1/2 cup butter and 1 cup powdered sugar together until smooth. Add 3 well beaten egg yolks, 1/2 tsp. vanilla and melted chocolate. Fold in stiffly beaten egg whites. Line 1/2 wafer mixture in a 9 inch pan. Spread with chocolate mixture. Cover with the remaining wafer mixture.

My photo/09

82

Peach Custard Tart

Mix 1/2 tsp. salt and 1 1/8 cup flour together, cut in 1/2 cup margarine until lumps are the size of peas. Blend in 2 tb. sour cream. Knead to form a dough, pat in and on sides of a 10 x 6 baking dish, bake at 425 for 10 minutes.

Mix 3 slightly beaten egg yolks, 1 cup sugar, 2 tb. flour and 1/3 cup sour cream until well blended. Arrange 4 cups freshly sliced peaches in hot crust, pour sour cream mixture over top. Cover with tin foil. Bake in a 350 oven for 35 minutes. Remove foil and bake 10 minutes more or until set. Serve warm.

My Photo/09

83

Frosty Sherbert Punch

Pour 3 cans 46 oz. chilled orange-grapefruit juice, 3 12 oz. cans chilled apricot nectar, 3 qts. chilled ginger ale into punch bowl. Add 1 qt. pineapple sherbet. Spoon liquid over sherbet until partially melted, serve. Repeat process as needed. 3 qt. sherbert makes 2 1/2 gallons

My Photo/09

Pie Crust and Toppings

Pies

The first pies were called " coffins or coffyns" the crust itself was the pan," the pastry was tough and inedible. The pastry shell was mainly used as a storage container and serving dish, and "often too hard to eat." In the 16th century cookbooks began to appear with pastry ingredients.

85 DINING CAR

My Photo/09

Plain Pastry Crust

Sift 1 1/2 cups flour, 1/2 tsp. salt together in a mixing bowl. Cut 1/2 cup shortening in with a pastry blender or blend with a fork.until mixture is in pieces about the size of peas. Add 4 to 5 tb. cold water, a few drops at a time, until mixture comes all together. Place mixture onto a sheet of wax paper. Gather up the corners of the paper, pressing from the outside to form a tight ball. Divide dough in two parts, for a top and bottom crust. Chill to let rest for 30 minutes. Roll pastry ball out on a floured board 1/8 inch thick. Roll lightly from center to outer edges. Place pastry in an 8 or 9 inch pie pan. Press lightly with fingertips to fit pan. Trim edges. Wet edge. Roll the upper crust. Transfer to a filled pie pan. Trim to fit, and press to seal tight with pressing with a wet fork or with your fingers.

Graham Cracker Crust

Combine 1 3/4 cup graham cracker crumbs, 1/4 cup finely chopped pecans, 1/2 tsp. cinnamon, 1/4 tsp. powdered ginger and 1/2 cup melted butter or margarine. Mix together well. Reserve 3 tb. of mixture. Press remainder on the bottom and up 2 1/2 inches up the sides of a 9 inch spring form pan. Use a smaller pan to press crumbs evenly. Fill with a cheesecake mixture. Use reserved mixture to sprinkle on top. Bake according to cheese cake recipe or use uncooked for pudding type pies.

Crumb Crust

Preheat oven at 375. Roll 20 square graham crackers between 2 sheets of wax paper. Crumbs should be fine and measure 1 2/3 cup. Mix in 1/4 cup softened butter or margarine with 1/4 cup sugar thoroughly, pour into a 9 inch pie plate. Use an 8 inch pie pan to press crumbs evenly up the sides and bottom. Bake 8 minutes.

My Photo/09

Rolled Oats Pie Crust

Set oven at 375. Combine 1 cup rolled oats, 1/3 cup sifted flour, 1/3 cup brown sugar and 1/2 tsp. salt in a mixing bowl. Add 1/3 cup melted margarine, mix until crumbly. Pack mixture firmly in bottom and on the sides of a 9 inch pie plate set a smaller pie plate inside to press evenly. Bake for 15 minutes. Let stand 5 minutes, remove smaller pan, cool crust. Fill with your choice of pie mixture.

My Photo/09

89

Tart Shells

Preheat oven to 450. Mix pastry for a 9 inch pie crust. use a 5 or 6 inch round cookie cutter to cut out circles. Fit evenly into large muffin pans, press down evenly and prick surface with a fork.. Crimp edge into decorative rim. Bake for 15 minutes. 90

My Photo/ 08

Pies, Bars and Squares

Apple Pie

In a large bowl combine 1 cup sugar, 1/2 tsp. powdered ginger, 1 tsp. cinnamon, 1/4 tsp. nutmeg, 1/4 tsp. salt, 2 tb. flour, 3 tb. strong tea and 1 tb. lemon juice. Mix well. Mix in 4 cups pared, cored and sliced apples, mix to coat evenly. Pour into pie crust until filled.

"Heap apples towards the center and dot with butter." Roll out top crust and cut slits for steam to escape, place over apples. Trim pastry and press edges together with a fork. Bake 40 to 50 minutes or until apples are tender and crust is browned. Cool slightly before slicing.

* Cut pastry ball in half and roll out 1/2 for bottom crust. Fit into a 9 inch pie pan. Set aside the remaining 1/2 of pastry for top crust. preheat oven at 425.

My Photo/09

Chocolate Pie

Prepare a 9 inch Graham crust. Melt a 19 oz. Hershey Almond Bar in a double boiler over boiling water. Stir in 2/3 cup milk and add 12 marshmallows, stir until smooth. Remove from heat and cool. Fold in 1 cup whipped heavy cream. Pour into the graham crumb shell, Chill. Serve with additional whipped cream on top.

Oops no chocolate ? you can substitute cocoa, 3 tb. cocoa plus 2 tb. vegetable shorting is equal to 1 oz. baking

93

1960 Mock Apple Pie

Ritz Crackers was celebrated their 75th birthday, by introducing their mock apple pie.

This recipe debuted in 1934 on the box. where it stayed through much of the 1960s. It last appeared in 1993." The pie became popular during the depression when apples were hard to come by. So crackers were used instead...

Mix 2 cups sugar and 2 tsp. cream of tarter in a sauce pan. Gradually stir in 1 3/4 cups water, bring to a boil on high heat, drop the heat to low and simmer on low for 15 minutes. Stir in the zest of 1 lemon and 2 tb. juice of lemon. Cool for 30 minutes. Heat oven at 425. Roll out half of a 2 crust plain pastry recipe on a lightly floured board to a 11 inch circle. Place in a 9 inch pie plate. Crush 36 Ritz Crackers, broken coarsely to make 3/4 cup.

Place in pie crust, pour sugar syrup over crackers.

Top with 2 tb. butter and 1/2 tsp. cinnamon. Roll out remaining pastry to a 10 inch circle, place over pie. Flute edges and poke with a fork threw crust to permit steam to escape. Bake for 30 to 35 minutes.

94

Impossible Pie

Place 4 eggs, 1/4 cup margarine, 1 cup sugar 1/2 cup flour, 1/4 tsp. salt, 1/2 tsp. baking powder, 2 cups milk, 1 cup shredded coconut, and 1 tsp. vanilla in a blender. Blend until mixed together evenly. Pour into a buttered 10 inch pie dish. Bake at 350 for 60 minutes. When done, crust will be at the bottom, the custard in the middle and coconut on the top. Just as where they belong.

Cindys beach/ Nics Bird
My Graphics

95

Deep Dish Blueberry Pie

Prepare a 2 crust 9 inch pastry shell. Roll out 1/2 of the pastry 1/4 inch thick and preheat the oven at 450.   Wash and drain 2 1/2 cups blueberries, pick out the blemished berries. In a bowl combine berries with 1 cup sugar, 1/4 cup flour, 1/8 tsp. salt and 1 tb. lemon juice. Mix evenly. Pour into the pastry shell. " Dot with 2 tb. margarine." "Roll out remaining pastry 1/4 inch thick, Pierce in several places with a fork. Cover berries with pastry, trim and crimp edges." Bake for 10 minutes then reduce heat to 350 and bake 30 minutes longer.   Cool slightly before cutting into wedges.

MY Photo/09

Raisin Pie

Set oven at 450. Combine 1 cup brown sugar, 2 tb. flour, 1/8 tsp salt, 1 cup raisins, 1 cup hot water and the juice of 1 lemon, mixing well after each addition. Cook in a saucepan until mixture thickens, Stirring to prevent scorching. "Cool and pour into an 8 inch pan lined with plain pastry. Cover with a top crust and bake for 10 minutes for then drop the heat to 350 for 35 minutes." Cool before slicing.

Butter Tarts

Beat 1 egg, gradually adding 1/2 cup brown sugar and 1/8 tsp. salt, 1 tsp. vanilla and 1 tsp. lemon juice. Beat until full of bubbles. Fold in 1/2 cup soaked and drained raisins and 1 tb.melted butter .

Drop mixture from a tsp. into a tart shell nested in a muffin tin. Bake in a 400 oven for 12 to 15 minutes or until the filling is set and pastry is golden brown

My Photo/09

Berry Pudding Pie

Bake a 10 inch crumb crust and fill it with fresh berries of choice or sliced peaches, about 3 cups. Pour over a vanilla pudding from the recipe on page 108. Pour over berries while still warm. Sprinkle with toasted chopped nuts.

My Photo/Garry's Bird

Banana Cheese Pie

Preheat oven at 350. "Slice 2 medium bananas. Blend 2 eggs." 1 cup yogurt, 1 cup low fat cottage cheese, juice from 1/2 a lemon and 1 tsp. vanilla in a blender on low speed. "Add 3 tb.honey then add the bananas." Pour into a crumb crust and bake for 25 to 30 minutes.Sprinkle with toasted coconut.

Garry's Photo/09

Peppermint Candy Tarts

Preheat oven to 350. "Grease a 32 mini muffin cups pan." "In a large bowl beat 1/2 cup sugar and 1/2 cup butter with a electric mixer on medium speed until fluffy. Beat in peppermint extract and blend in 1 egg. Blend in 1 1/2 cup flour and 1/4 tsp. baking soda.

Shape dough into 1 1/2 inch balls and press each into the bottom and sides of muffin tins. Bake for 9 to 12 minutes until edges are golden brown. Cool for 1 minute and remove to a cooling rack for 15 minutes. In a bowl, combine 2 cups powdered sugar, 3 tb. soften butter, 2 drops red food color and 2 to 3 tb. milk. Beat on medium speed until smooth and creamy." Stir in 1/4 cup crushed hard peppermint candies.

Spoon 1 round measuring teaspoon of filling into each tart shell. Sprinkle with crushed candies.

My Photo/10

Easy Meat Pie

"Cook 1 lb. ground beef, 1 small chopped onion in a skillet until meat has cooked through, drain." Add 1 11 oz. can undiluted condensed beef with vegetables and barley soup, and 1 10 oz. can undiluted condensed golden mushroom soap," 3 medium uncooked 1/2 inch cubed potatoes, 4 medium sliced carrots 1/8 thick, 1/4 tsp. salt and pepper mix well. Divide into 2 ungreased 9 inch pie plates. Roll out plain pastry on a floured board to fit the top of each pie and place over filling." Seal and flute edges, cut slits to release steam. Bake at 350 for 45 to 50 minutes or until golden brown. Let cool on a wire rack for 15 minutes before serving.

To make a chicken pie, cook 1 lb. cubed chicken with onion, add 1 can chicken vegetable soup and 1 can cream chicken instead of the beef vegetable and cream mushroom. then fallow recipe.

101

My Photo/08

Oat Chocolate Chip Squares

"In a bowl combine 1 cup flour, 1 cup rolled oats and 3/4 cup brown sugar." Cut in 1/2 cup cold margarine or butter until crumbly. Press half of the mixture into a greased 13 x 9 inch baking pan. Bake at 350 for 8 to 10 minutes. Remove from oven." Spread 1 14 oz can. sweetened condensed milk evenly over crust, sprinkle with 1 cup chopped pecans and 1 cup chocolate chips. Top with remaining oat mixture, pat lightly. Bake for 25 to 30 minutes or until lightly browned. Cool in pan on a wire rack.

Old Fashioned O' Henry Bars

Melt 3/4 cup peanut butter, 3/4 cup corn syrup and 3/4 cup brown sugar in a double boiler. Add 1 1/2 cup peanuts and 1 1/2 cup rice krispies and mix well. Pack into a 8x8 greased pan. Cool for 20 minutes and cut into bars. Cool completely in fridge.

Chocolate Coating

Combine 1/4 square paraffin wax and 1 1/2 cup chocolate chips in a double boiler until completely melted. Dip bars into mixture, use a pic when dipping. Place on wax paper to cool.

Cindy's Photo/07

Lemon Crumble Squares

"Preheat at 350." In a mixing bowl add 1 cup self raising flour, rub in 3/4 cup butter until crumbly. Add 3/4 cup castor sugar, 1/2 tsp. chopped candied citron peel, 2 eggs and 3 tb. lemon juice to make a sticky consistency. "Scrape into a greased and floured 8 inch square pan." Spread out evenly.

Crumble........Rub 2 tb. butter and 1/4 cup flour together. Add 1/4 cup sugar, and the rind from 2 lemons. Spread the uncooked cake with marmalade. Sprinkle the crumble on top and bake for 45 minutes.

Nic's Photo/ 09

Almond Squares

Mix together 1/2 cup margarine, 1 cup brown sugar, 3 egg yolks, 1 1/2 cup flour, 1 tsp. baking powder, 1 tsp. salt and 1 tsp. vanilla. Pat into a greased pan. Beat 2 eggs whites until foamy, gradually add 1 cup brown sugar and beat until stiff peaks form. Spread on top of mixture. Sprinkle with 1/2 cup flaked almonds and bake in a preheated oven at 325 for 25 to 30 minutes. Cool and cut into squares.

My Photo/07
Garry's Duck/08

Nanaimo Squares

Heat 1/2 cup margarine, 1/4 cup sugar and 3 tb. cocoa in a double boiler, stir until smooth. Add 1 beaten egg and 1 tsp. vanilla stir to mix evenly. Remove from heat and add 2 cups graham cracker crumbs. Spread mixture in an 8x8 pan and place in refrigerator to set. Cream 1/4 cup butter, 2 cups icing sugar, 2 tb. custard powder, and 2 tb. milk. Spread over the set mixture and return to refrigerator to set. "Lastly, melt 2 squares chocolate with 1 tsp. butter in a double boiler. while hot spread very thinly over the set mixture and refrigerate once again." After setting cut into small squares and serve cold.

My Photo/09

"Pistachios Fruit Chocolate Chip Bars"

Preheat oven at 325. Combine 2 cups flour, 1 1/4 cups uncooked oats, 1 cup packed dark brown sugar, 1/2 tsp. cinnamon, and 1/2 tsp. salt with a electric mixer on low speed beat. until well combined. Add 1 cup chilled butter, cut into 1/2 inch chunks. Mix on medium speed until blended and appears moist and begins to pulls together, about 3 minutes. Mix in 1 cup chopped and shelled pistachios. Reserve 1 1/2 cups of this crumb mixture. Stir in 1/2 cup dried and diced apricots and 1/2 cup chocolate chips into mixture and refrigerate. Firmly press the remaining mixture into the bottom of an ungreased 13 x9 inch baking pan. Bake for 25 minutes in a 350 oven.   Cool for 20 minutes.

Spread a 15 oz. jar of apricot preserves evenly on top, leaving a boarder around the edge of the crust. Sprinkle the reserved crumb mixture over the top. Bake until lightly browned and bubbly and the fruit filling spreads all over, 35 to 40 minutes. Cool before slicing into bars.

My Photos/08

Desserts and Puddings

Vanilla Pudding Surprise

In a sauce pan beat 3 eggs . Stir in 1/2 cup sugar and 1/4 tsp. salt. Gradually blend in 1 3/4 cup milk into egg mixture. Cook, stirring constantly, over low heat until mixture thickens slightly and will coat a spoon. Remove from heat, stir in 1/2 tsp. vanilla. Fold in 1 cup sour cream. Cool before serving. 108

My Photo/09

RADIO PUDDING

Recipe from rural Canada in 1900. This one came on the radio, Gram didn't catch the name, so she called it radio pudding.

In a saucepan add 2 cups boiling water, 1 cup brown sugar, 1 tb. butter and a pinch salt, bring to a boil on a medium heat. Stir in 1 tb. flour dissolved in 1 cup cold water keep stirring until thickened, set aside and keep warm. In a bowl mix together 1 cup flour, 2 tsp. baking powder, 1 tb. butter, 1/2 cup raisins and 1/2 cup milk, mix just well enough to incorporate. Drop by a spoon into the syrup mixture as dumplings and bake in a 350 oven for 20 minutes or until golden brown.

My Photo/ 07

Butterscotch Bananas

In a sauce pan cook together 1/2 cup corn syrup, 1/2 cup brown sugar, 2 tb. light cream and 2 tb. butter stirring until sugar has dissolved. Bubble for 5 minutes, and cool then add 1 tsp. vanilla. Pour over slices of bananas. Top with whipped cream.

My Photo/09

Grandmas Peach Cobbler

"Melt 1/2 cup butter in a 9x13 inch ovenproof dish in a preheated oven at 350". "In a bowl mix" together 1 cup flour, 1 1/2 tsp. baking powder, 1/2 tsp. salt, 3/4 cup sugar and 1 cup milk. When butter has melted spread batter into prepared oven dish. Then carefully spoon 1 can of peaches with juice evenly over the batter. Return to oven and bake 30 minutes. The batter will rise around the peaches.

My morning visitor 09

111

Tutti Frutti Dessert

Pour 3 cups of an assortment or 1 kind of canned fruit in a buttered shallow baking dish. Sift 3/4 cup flour, 3/4 cup sugar, 1 tsp. baking powder and 1/2 tsp. salt together in a bowl. Add 1 unbeaten egg and 1/2 cup yogurt, mix well. Then spread evenly over fruit. Bake at 375 for 30 minutes or until golden brown. Serve with icecream.

My Photo/09

Five Cup Dessert

Combine 1 cup cooked rice, 1 cup canned crushed pineapple, 1 cup mini mashmallows, 1 cup chopped walnuts and 1 cup whipped cream, in the order listed. Chill thoroughly before serving.

My Photo/09

Apple Walnut Cobbler

Peel and slice 4 cups apples, arrange in a buttered casserole dish, "set aside". In a bowl combine 1/2 cup sugar, 1/2 tsp. cinnamon, 1/2 coarsely chopped walnuts. Sprinkle over apples. Combine 1 cup flour, 1 tsp. baking powder, 1/4 tsp. salt, stir well and set aside. Combine 1 beaten egg, 1 cup milk and 1/3 cup melted butter, mix together well. Add flour mixture beating until smooth. Pour over apples. Combine 1/4 cup finely chopped walnuts, and cinnamon sugar, sprinkle over batter. Bake in a 325 oven

Garrys Photo/09

114

Caramel Apple Pudding

"Melt 24 caramels with 1/4 cup water in a double boiler over a low heat, stirring until sauce is smooth". Place 4 cups bread cubes in a greased casserole dish. Top with 4 cups peeled and sliced apples. Combine 2 cups milk, 1/4 cup sugar, 1 tsp. vanilla, 1/4 tsp. salt, 1/4 tsp. cinnamon and 4 slightly beaten eggs, stir to mix. Pour over apples. Cover with caramel sauce. Set dish in large pan, pour in boiling water 1/2 inch deep. Bake in a 325 oven for 1 1/2 hour or until a inserted knife comes out clean.

Nic's Photo/ 08

Peanut Butter and Jam pudding

Preheat oven at 350. Grease a casserole dish, melt 3 tb. butter with 2/3 cup peanutbutter on low heat until a smooth mixture forms. Mix 1 3/4 cup milk, add 4 beaten eggs, 1/3 cup sugar, 2 tsp. vanilla. Place 6 cups cubed bread in greased casserole dish. Pour over the milk and egg mixture, let stand for 10 minutes, Dollop with strawberry or raspberry jam press in slightly to incorporate the mixture, Sprinkle with sugar on top. Place in a large pan with water half up, bake oven for 50 to 60 minutes or until set.

116

Garry's Photo/10

Indian Pudding

"Scald 3 cups milk and 1/3 cup dark molasses over low heat." Stir in 1/3 cup cornmeal, whisk until slightly thickened, about 10 minutes. Together combine 1 large egg, 1/4 cup sugar, 1/2 tsp. cinnamon, 1/2 tsp. grated orange peel and 1/4 tsp. salt in a buttered large casserole dish. Gradually mix in the hot cornmeal. Bake in a 300 oven for 45 minutes. Cool on a wire rack.

Topping Sauce

In a small bowl cream 1/3 cup butter with an electric mixer, beat in 1 cup sifted icing sugar until mixture is light. "Beat in 1/4 cup heavy cream and 1/2 tsp. vanilla. Pour over top of pudding."

117

Floating Island

Preheat oven at 350. Heat 2 cups milk until film forms across top. Beat 3 egg yolks until bubbly, stir in 1/4 cup sugar and 1/4 tsp. salt. Slowly add milk slowly to egg yolks. Place mixture over hot water, cook, stirring constantly, until thickens and coats a spoon.

Remove and chill for 2 to 3 hours. Beat 3 egg whites until stiff, add 1/4 cup sugar a little at a time, add 1/4 tsp vanilla." Spoon beaten egg whites on top in mounds, making floating Islands."
Bake for 25 minutes.

118

Cookies

My Photo/08

The Cookie Will Travel

When people started to explore the globe, biscuits became the ideal traveling food. They stayed fresh for long periods of time, and proved to be portable and had a long storage life. The English, Scotch and Dutch immigrants originally brought the first cookies to America.

Digestive Cookies

Sift 1 1/2 cups flour, 2 tsp. baking powder, 1/2 tsp. salt and 1/4 cup sugar. Mix in 1/4 cup oatmeal and rub in 3 tb. lard or margarine. Add just enough milk to form a firm dough. Knead on a floured board. Roll out thinly, prick with a fork and cut into rounds. Bake on a greased baking sheet at 400 for 15 minutes or just until golden.

Orange Shortbread Cookies

Mix together 4 cups flour, 1/4 tsp. salt, 1 cup packed brown sugar and 1 tb. grated orange rind. Mix in 1 cup butter until smooth. Chill for 1 hour. On a floured board roll out dough 1/2 inch thick. Cut out with a floured cookie cutter. Brush with 1 beaten egg white and sprinkle with little candies. Bake at 350 on a baking tray for 15 to 20 minutes.

121

My Photo/08

cookie Jam Logs

In a large bowl cream together 1 pkg. of cream cheese, 1/2 cup soft butter and 2/3 cup sugar with an electric mixer on medium speed until blended well. Separate 1 egg and set egg white aside. Add 1 whole egg and the egg yolk with 1 tsp. vanilla into the cream cheese mixture, mix well.

In another bowl mix together 2 1/2 cups flour and 1/2 tsp. baking powder. Gradually blend in flour mixture to the cream cheese mixture after each addition mix in well until all blended. Divide dough into 4 equal pieces. Roll into 1 x12 inch log. Place 2 inches apart on a large ungreased baking sheet. Make a depression down the length of the log with the handle of a wooden spoon about 1/2 inch wide and 1/2 inch deep. Beat reserved egg white with a fork, brush over each log. Sprinkle with 1/3 cup finely chopped walnuts. Warm 3/4 cup strawberry jam in microwave for 30 seconds. Fill depression with jam using 3 tb. for each log. Bake in a 350 preheated oven for 25 to 27 minutes, until lightly browned. Transfer to a wire rack to cool.

122

My Photo/09

Buffalo Chip Cookies

Preheat oven to 350. In a large bowl, cream 1 cup butter, 1 cup of Crisco, 2 cups brown sugar and 2 cups white sugar. Add 4 eggs and 2 tsp. vanilla. Sift together 4 cups flour, 2 tsp. baking powder, 2 tsp. baking soda, 1 tsp. salt. Then add 2 cups oatmeal, 1 10 oz. pkg. chocolate chips, 1 cup chopped pecans, 2 cups Rice Krispies cereal, and 1 cup coconut. Mix into egg mixture. Use a large scoop and place dough on a ungreased cookie sheet. Bake for 12 minutes at 350. Cool for 3 minutes, move to a wire rack.

Garry's Photo/08

Peaches and Cream Cookies

Beat 1 cup shortening and 1 1/2 cups sugar together. Blend in 2 eggs and 1 cup chopped fresh peaches into sugar mixture. In another bowl mix together 3 cups flour, 1 tsp. salt, 1/2 tsp. baking soda and 3/4 cup chopped walnuts. Stir and blend into sugar mixture and mix well. Drop dough by the tsp. on to a greased cookie sheet. Cookies will double in size while baking so set far apart from each other. Bake in a preheated oven to 325 for 12 to 15 minutes.

Parkin Cookies

Cream 1/2 cup lard, add 2 eggs and beat well. beat in 1 cup molasses. Sift together 1 1/2 cups flour, 1 tsp salt, 1 tsp. baking soda, 1 tsp cinnamon, 1/2 tsp. cloves. Add 1/2 cup rolled oats. Blend in to the egg mixture, add 1 cup raisins.

Drop from a tsp. onto a greased cookie sheet. Bake in a preheated oven to 375 for 25 minutes.

My Photo/09

Whole Wheat Cookie Crackers

In a bowl mix together 2/3 cup oat flour, (If using rolled oats blend in blender until fine) 1 1/2 cups whole wheat flour and 1/2 tsp. salt. Rub 6 tb. butter with hands into flour mixture until crumbly.. Mix in 2 tb.honey along with milk just enough to hold dough together in a ball. Place on a cookie sheet and spread out, roll with a floured rolling pin until 1/4 inch thick. Prick with a fork all over, cut into wedges. Bake in a 350 oven for 25 minutes. Slide onto a wire rack.

My Photo/ 09

Sugar and Spice Cookies

Sift together 2 1/2 cups flour, 1/8 tsp. salt, 1/2 tsp. cream of tarter, 1/2 tsp. baking soda, 1/2 tsp. nutmeg, 1/4 tsp. cinnamon. In a large bowl cream together 1/4 cup shorting, 1/4 cup butter, 1 cup sugar until light and fluffy. Beat in 1 egg and 1/3 cup milk. Stir in flour mixture. Chill for 3 to 4 hours. Roll dough on a floured board about 1/4 inch thick, cut with a floured cookie cutter. Place on a greased cookie sheet. Brush lightly with 1 beaten egg white and sprinkle with sugar. Bake in a 375 oven for 10 to 12 minutes.

Nut Crisps

Cream 1/4 cup butter, add 1/2 cup sugar, cream until light and fluffy. Add 1 egg and mix well. Sift 1 cup whole wheat flour 5 times. Add 1 tsp. baking powder, 1/4 tsp. salt and sift again. Fold into butter mixture, and add 1/4 tsp. vanilla. Set in refrigerator and chill for 35 minutes. Roll into small balls, place on a greased baking sheet, press flat with a wet fork. Place half a peanut meat on top of each crisp. Bake in a 375 oven for 10 to 12 minutes.

Bird's Nest Cookies

Cream together 1 cup butter, 1/2 cup sugar and 1/4 tsp. salt until light and fluffy. Add 1 1/2 tsp. vanilla and 2 egg yolks, 1 at a time, beating after each addition. Stir in 2 cups flour, mix thoroughly. Shape into balls. Dip into slightly beaten egg whites, then roll in 1 cup chopped nuts. Place on an ungreased baking sheet about 1 inch apart make a depression in the center of each cookie.

Bake in a 375 oven for 15 minutes, remove from oven and before the cookies cool, press chocolate bits in the centers.

Linda Nicola's Photo/09

Melting Moments

Beat 2/3 cup butter with 2/3 cup sugar.

Add 2 eggs and beat until light and fluffy.

Sift together 1 cup flour, 1/2 cup cornstarch,

2 tsp. baking powder. Stir into butter mixture.

Add 1 tsp. grated lemon rind and 1 cup roasted

chopped almonds. Drop mixture from a tsp. on a

greased baking sheet 2 inches apart. Bake in a

350 preheated oven for 10 to 12 minutes.

Garry's Photo/09

Granola Chewies

In a sauce pan melt 1/2 cup butter or margarine, mix in 2/3 cup firmly packed dark brown sugar, add 1/3 cup honey. Turn into a 2 quart bowl, mix in 1 1/2 cups old-fashioned rolled oats, 1 cup finely chopped apricots, 1/2 cup chopped almonds, 1/2 cup wheat germ and 1/2 cup dried cranberries.Mix together well with hands, form into 1 inch diameter balls. Place balls on a greased baking sheet and bake in a 300 oven for 10 minutes.

131

Dutch Cookies

Sift together 2 2/3 cups unsifted cake and pastry flour, 1 tsp. cinnamon, 1/2 tsp. baking soda, 1/4 tsp. salt, knead in 1 cup butter or margarine and 1 cup firmly packed brown sugar. Add 1/2 tsp. almond extract. Divide dough in half and press out thinly on 2 ungreased cookie sheet evenly. Beat 1 egg and add 1 tsp cold water, brush over dough. Sprinkle with 1/2 cup chopped or slivered almonds with 1/3 cup sugar evenly, Bake at 350 for 15 to 17 minutes. Cool 2 minutes then cut into 4x2 rectangles.

Ragged Robins

Cream 1 cup soft butter with 2 cups brown sugar. Add 2 eggs. Sift together 2 cups flour, 2 tsp. baking soda, 1/2 tsp. salt. Add to butter mixture along with 1 cup chopped walnuts, 1/2 cup finely chopped mixed candied fruit, 1 tsp. vanilla and 2 tb. water. Drop by spoonfuls onto a greased cookie sheet, center with 1/2 of a Maraschino cherry and bake at 350 for 12 minutes or until lightly browned.

notes

Store cottage cheese upside down and it will keep longer.

What no soda? Serve 1/2 fruit juice and 1/2 salt free seltzer, have the fizzy taste without the sugar or salt in soda.

Peel a narrow strip of skin all around the middle of an apple, It won't shrink much during baking

Dipping slices of bacon in flour and cooking over low heat will keep it from curling.

When baking potatoes for a crowd, rub the skins with margarine or butter and add salt and pepper. Bake in muffin tins to avoid burned fingers when pulling them out of the

Core and slice apples 1/4 inch thick, sprinkle lightly with a sugar-cinnamon mixture. Saute in butter over low heat. Use as a side dish for pork or chicken.

For a tasty treat blend peanut butter in softened vanilla ice cream, spread between a graham crackers and freeze make a tasty treat.

If you find your home made soup to salty, all you have to do is add a slice of raw potato and cook for a few minutes longer, the potato will absorb the excess salt

When planning a meat loaf make a 1 serving loaf by using a muffin tin. Extras can be frozen for an easy meal for later.

Vegetables wrapped in paper towelling before storing will stay fresh and rust free .

" For tender asparagus from top to bottom, peel the bottoms with a potato peeler It will taste just as good as the tops."

Even in cool weather never let food sit out on the table for more than 2 hours.

"Romaine has more vitamins than Iceberg lettuce."

Flour thickened gravies need to cook long enough to remove the raw flour taste.

"Remove bread from the pan as soon as it's taken from the oven."

"Thump the top of the loaf, if it sounds hollow, it's done."

"A roast with a bone will cook faster then a boneless roast. The bone will carry heat."

"Use the fruit juice from canned or frozen fruit instead of water in your recipe."

"Store celery in foil. It will keep in the refrigerator for weeks."

"You'll double the juice of a lemon if you microwave it for 10 seconds before squeezing."

"Skin on garlic cloves slip off if you microwave it for 10 seconds."

"Always add the chocolate chips to the cookie mix last. It's best when they are cold and barely stir in, don't over mix."

"Lettuce keeps better in your refrigerator without washing. Keep in a tightly sealed container. Wash just what will be used right away".

"No more than 3 herbs and spices in 1 dish, is the exception to the rule."

"When preparing long cooking meals, add herbs and spices during the last hour. Cooking spices too long will result in an overly overly strong flavor."

Salt, pepper, garlic and cayenne are a good mix.

"Add macaroni to rapidly boiling water with a lump of butter. Loosen with a fork, turn off burner and cover. Let stand for 20 minutes to make perfect macaroni."

Use a little yellow food color and a tsp. of lemon juice in fruit pies. Lemon will enhance flavor and keep a bright color

Cinnamon, nutmeg, cloves and allspice are meant for sweet dishes.

Place a slice of dry bread on top of fully cooked and drained rice and cover. The bread will absorb moisture, leaving the rice fluffy and dry.

"Adding 1/2 cup cold water to 1 lb. ground beef before grilling makes a juicer burger"

"Basil hates to be cold, store it in a glass with the water level covering only the stems, and change the water occasionally. I will even develop roots. Regular cutting encourages a new growth."

countryside Dinners

Roast Duck with Honey Curry

Puncture all over with a fork 1 large or 2 small ducks that have been washed and cleaned. Rub the duck with a mixture of thyme, salt and pepper. Place on back in a broiler pan on a rack. Bake at a 325 oven for 1 1/2 to 2 hours, until skin becomes a light brown and crisp. While roasting mix together 4 tb. slightly heated honey and 1 1/2 tsp. curry powder. Brush mixture on every 10 minutes until crisped and browned. If glaze is still sticky, place briefly under the broiler with a very close eye, so as not to burn. Little black spots is still good.

137

Garry's photo/09

Onion and Sausage Pie

In a skillet melt 2 tb. margarine, add 1 large peeled and diced potato, add 1 link of smoked sausage sliced and diced, saute until browned. Add 1 cup frozen corn, 1 cup frozen peas, and 1 can small baby small onions. Cook, stirring until mixture has evenly browned, about 8 to 10 minutes.   Mix in 1 can mushroom soup evenly, simmer and stir just enough to evenly mix.   Add water if needed to keep smooth.
Turn into a ready made pie crust and top with a pie crust. Brush with an egg wash. Bake in a 350 oven for 15 to 25 minutes or until golden brown.

Nic's Photo/ 09

Easy Veal Goulash

Saute 4 cubed veal steaks in 2 tb. of butter in a large frying pan for 3 minutes and turn. Brown other side; remove from pan and keep warm. Stir in 2 cups chopped onions. Add 2 tb. butter, cover and cook until onions are tender, about 5 minutes. Sprinkle in 2 tb. flour, 1 tb. paprika, 1 tsp. salt, 1 tsp. marjoram on top; blend in evenly. Stir in 1 can stewed tomatoes, and 1/2 cup water. Simmer at a low boil for 1 minute, stirring constantly until sauce thickens. Add veal and heat on a slow boil. Spoon over noodles.

Veal Piccata

Dip 1 1/2 lb. veal in a plate of flour, tap off any excess. Heat 2 tb. butter and oil in a large skillet. Brown on each side, turning once. Add more butter if needed. Remove to a warm plate. Pour in 1 cup water and 1 tsp. chicken broth, stir to gather all browning. Grate in the rind from 1 lemon and squeeze in the juice from the lemon. Return veal to the skillet and simmer covered for 15 minutes. Serve with slice of lemon

140

My Photo/08

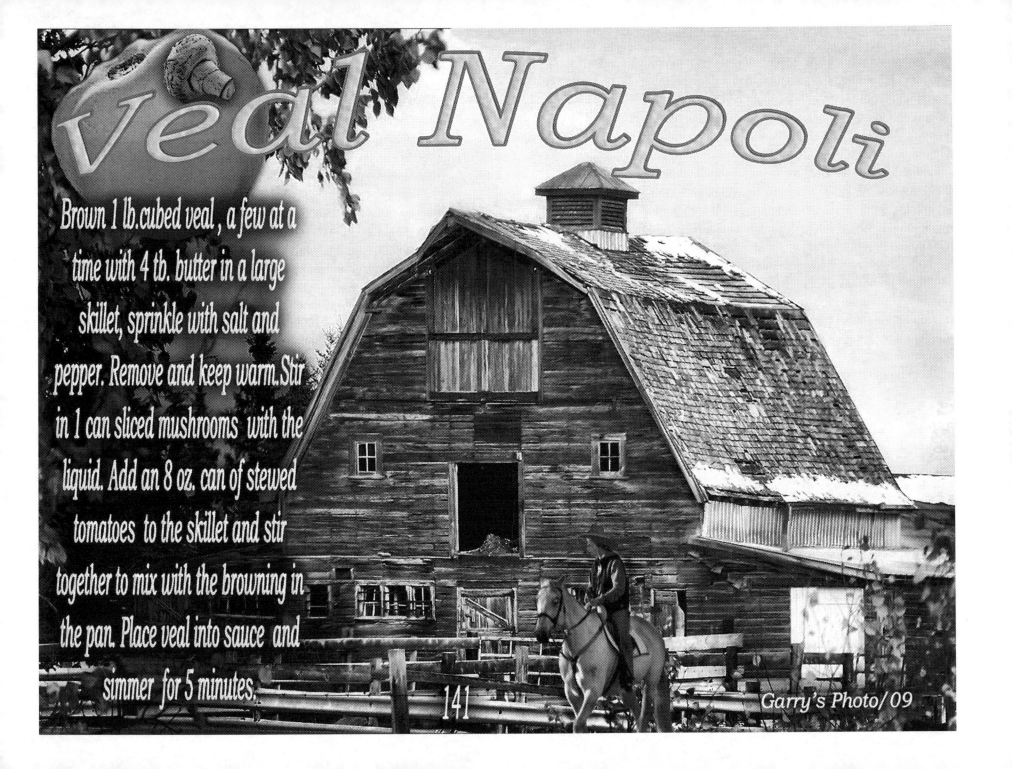

Veal Napoli

Brown 1 lb. cubed veal, a few at a time with 4 tb. butter in a large skillet, sprinkle with salt and pepper. Remove and keep warm. Stir in 1 can sliced mushrooms with the liquid. Add an 8 oz. can of stewed tomatoes to the skillet and stir together to mix with the browning in the pan. Place veal into sauce and simmer for 5 minutes.

141

Garry's Photo/ 09

Creole Succotash

Cook 1 pkg. 10 oz. frozen baby lima beans following label directions. When almost tender add 1 pkg. 10 oz. frozen whole kernel corn. Heat to a boiling point, lower heat and simmer for 2 minutes. If needed add 1 or 2 tb. of water to finish cooking, water should be absorbed when done. Stir in 1 can stewed tomatoes, heat until steaming and top with butter.

Nic's Photo
Garry's Bee

Spicy Sauce Roast Pork

Salt and pepper a 4 to 5 lb. fresh picnic shoulder pork roast, and place fat side up on a rack in an open roaster. Roast at 350 for 40 to 45 minutes per pound. In a saucepan mix together 2 small minced onions, 1 tb. Worcestershire sauce, 1 cup sugar, 1/2 tsp. paprika, 1/2 cup vinegar, 1/2 cup water, and 2 tb. catsup, cook for 5 minutes. Pour over roast and serve

143

My Photos

Hawaiian Baked Pork

Preheat oven at 350. Place 2 cups crushed unsweetened pineapple in a large baking dish. Peel 3 medium size sweet potatoes and place slices over pineapple, sprinkle 1 cup brown sugar on top. Season 4 pork steaks with salt and pepper. Place steaks on top of potatoes. Arrange 4 bacon strips on top of pork. Cover and bake for 1 hour. Remove cover and increase temperature to 450 for the last 10 to 15 minutes to brown the steak and bacon.

Garry's Photo

Pigs in Potatoes

Place 6 small sausage links in a heavy skillet, add 1/4 cup water, cover and steam for 5 minutes. Drain off water and cook and brown for 10 to 15 minutes. Beat 2 cups cold mashed potatoes, 1 egg yolk, 1 tb. finely chopped onion and 1 tsp. finely chopped parsley. Then coat each cooked sausage with the mixture, roll in 1/4 cup fine dry bread crumbs, then in 1 tb. water diluted egg, then again in bread crumbs. Fry sausages in 2 tb. very hot oil until golden brown.

145

Nic's Cowboy –

My Photo

The oven Wonder

Mix 1 1/4 cup long grain rice, 1 envelope of dry vegetable soup mix together in a greased small roasting pan. Mix together 1 can of condensed cream of mushroom soup with 1 can condensed cream of asparagus soup along with 2 cups water in a bowl until smooth. Pour over rice and stir well. Bake uncovered in a 375 oven for 45 minutes, Stir well. Brown 8 small boneless pork chops in 2 batches, in cooking oil in a skillet on medium high heat until browned on each side.

Place pork on top of rice. Push down into liquid. Cover and bake 45 to 60 minutes.

My Photo/ 09

Porcupine Meat Balls

Combine together 1 lb. lean ground beef, 1/2 cup uncooked rice, 1 tsp. salt, 1/8 tsp. pepper and 2/3 cup tomato paste. Mix well. Form into 8 balls. In a large skillet melt 2 tb. margarine and brown on all sides. Remove to a casserole dish and add 1 onion, cut in rings, 1 cup tomato sauce, 1 cup diced celery and 1 diced green pepper. Combine 1 tsp.salt, 1/2 tsp. dry mustard and 1 tb. sugar in 1/4 hot water.Pour over meat balls and cover.

Bake in a 350 oven for 45 to 50 minutes.

Moose Meatballs

In a bowl combine 1 lb. ground moose meat or ground beef in a bowl, 1 egg, 1 tb. cornstarch, 1 tsp. salt, 1/4 tsp pepper, and 2 tb. chopped onion. Shape into 1 1/2 inch balls. Brown in a large skillet with 1 tb. oil. Cover and simmer on low heat until, cooked about ten minutes. In a sauce pan mix together 3 tb. vinegar, 2 tb. cornstarch until smooth. Drain 1 8 oz. can of pineapple chunks. Reserve juice set pineapple aside. Add enough water to juice to make 1 1/2 cups. Stir into vinegar mixture. Add 1/2 cup sugar, 1 tb.soy sauce, stir and cook over medium heat until thickened. Add the meat balls, pineapple and 1 medium green pepper cut in strips. Cook until heated through. Serve over noodles.

148

Garry's Photo/09

Beef Stock

Prepare together 1 stick of celery, 1 large chopped carrot, 1 garlic clove cut in half, 1 large onion quartered, 1 bay leaf and set aside.

Trim excess fat from 4 lb. meaty oxtails. Place bones in a roasting pan and roast in a preheated oven at 425 until browned. Stir to turn over. Add vegetables, continue roasting for another 20 to 30 minutes or until it starts to caramelize. Take from oven and add 1 cup water, stir with a wooden spoon to blend all the browning. Place the mixture in a large stock pot with 15 cups water and 1 tb. tomato paste. Bring to a boil. Reduce heat and simmer for 2 more hours, scrape away the scum from the top as it simmers. Remove bones and set aside to cool. Strain stock and refrigerate overnight in 2 batches uncovered and stir every so often. When bones are cool remove meat for soups. Next morning remove stock from fridge, scrape any fat that has risen and solidified on top. The beef stock is now ready for soup. This makes 12 cups, Enough for 3 batches of soup for 4 people. Freeze what cannot be used in 3 days.

My Photos/09

149

Vegetable Stock

In a stock pot add 3 chopped carrots, 3 chopped celery stalks, 1 chopped potato, 1 quartered onion, 2 cloves garlic cut in half, 2 bay leaves, 5 whole peppercorn, salt and pepper to taste. Cover with water and bring to a boil. Lower heat to a simmer for 1 hour and strain. Discard the vegetables.

Roux

Heat 1 cup margarine or oil in a large skillet. Add 2 cups flour, stirring constantly. Cook for 5 to 6 minutes on medium heat. Will be slightly crumbly and a light brown color. Cool and refrigerate for up to 2 weeks. Use a spoon or 2 to thicken sauces, stews and soups.

My photo

Oriental Pork With Noodles

In a blender or food processor fitted with a steal blade combine 1/2 cup chicken broth, 1/3 cup creamy peanut butter, 2 tb. soy sauce, 1 1/2 tbs. vinegar, 1 tsp. sesame oil, 1 clove of garlic, 1/2 tsp. grated fresh ginger and 1/2 tsp. hot pepper sauce. Whirl until smooth. Cook 4 oz. egg noodles, toss 4 oz. fine egg noodles, drained and rinsed with water then tossed with 4 cups of stir fried finely shredded cabbage. Blanch 1/4 pound snow peas and julienne cut into matchsticks. Also julienne cut 1 medium size red bell pepper. In a large bowl combine the egg noodles and cabbage mixture, snow peas and pepper with 1/2 lb. cooked lean chopped boneless pork and 1 thinly sliced green onion, Add the dressing and toss to coat well.

Chicken Slice with Pineapple

Heat wok and add 2 tb. oil. Brown 12 oz. sliced chicken breast brown slightly and add 1 small green pepper and 1 small red pepper cut in squares, 1/2 tsp. minced garlic, 1/2 tsp. minced ginger and 1 8 oz. can pineapple chunks. Saute for 4 minutes and add 3 thinly sliced green onion. Then add 1 tb. Worchestershire sauce, 1 tb. oyster sauce, 1 tb. vinegar, 1 tsp. soy sauce and 1/4 cup water. Mix well and serve when hot.

151

My photo/08

Canadian History Notes

The first permanent settler of Canada was Louis Hebert in 1627

The first newspaper was printed in 1752, March 23 in Halifax which is still operation today.

In 1793 Attorney General John White, pasted the first bill the Prohibited the import of slaves into Upper Canada became the only British Colony to legislate for abolition slavery

The first Hudson's Bay Company, Beaver on the Pacific coast, visits Fort Vancouver in 1836

In 1838 the Durham Report, recommending united Canada under one Parliament as a solution to rebellion grievance was issued in London

In 1849 the Hudson's Bay Co. leases Vancouver Island for 7 shillings per year.

In 1858 there was announcement that Ottawa will be the new capital.

Early pioneers used basketful of eggs, often for a bartering tool for other foods consumptions.

A shopping list in 1880 to 1890 included sugar, tea, flour, baking soda, salt, oatmeal, rice, syrup, dried apples and coffee.

Coffee was often bought in the early pioneer time in green coffee beans and roasted their own. Roasted barley was put through a food chopper was a substitute for coffee.

In 1885 the CPR telegraph system was completed from coast to coast.

Furs and Coins were the main currency used in Canada in 1887 Ottawa issued the most colorful money in the world with the 1 dollar, 2 dollar, 50 dollar, and 1000 dollar .

The first Doukobors Immigrants from Russian religion arrived in Halifax in 1899

Potato, Macaroni Casserole

Peel, dice and cook 4 to 5 potatoes, drain and mash. Add butter, salt and pepper to taste. Boil 2 cups macaroni until almost cooked through, add butter and stir. Set both aside. In a skillet brown 1 lb. ground beef with 1 onion minced, salt and pepper to taste. Drain any fat. Add 1 can tomato soup, 1 small can diced tomato. Mix in the macaroni, pour mixture into a greased casserole dish, top with the mashed potato and cover completely. Top with 1 cup shredded cheddar cheese and bake in a 350 oven until cheese has melted and slightly browned.

153

My Photo/09

Potato Sausage Pudding

Slice 2 to 3 links of smoked sausage into rings, Saute with 1 large sliced onion in 1/4 cup butter until golden brown. Combine with 4 large baked, peeled and shredded potatoes. Add 1 peeled and shredded carrot and 2 beaten eggs with 2 tb. dry bread crumbs, 1 tsp.salt and 1/4 tsp. pepper. Turn into a greased casserole dish, cover. Bake at 350 for 1 hour and 15 minutes.

My Photo/09

Stewed Steak and Dumplings

Cube 1 1/2 lb. chuck steak. Heat a sauce pan with 1 tb. cooking oil and fry the meat for 2 minutes. Peel and cut into chunks a mixture of onions, carrots, turnip, celery and potatoes. Add 2 to 3 bouillon cubes mixed in 2 1/2 cups of water to the meat and bring to a boil. Season with herbs and salt and pepper to taste. Cook slowly for 2 1/2 hours until meat is tender. Thicken with a mixture of flour and some stock mixed together.

Simmer until thickened.

Dumplings.........Make sure there is plenty of stock in the stew pot before add the dumplings, as they absorb liquid.. Mix together 2 cups flour, 4 tsp. baking powder and 1 tsp. salt in a mixing bowl, cut in 2 tb. margarine until crumbly. Mix in 3/4 cup of water or milk just until mixed evenly. Drop dough from a tb. on to simmering stew. Cover stew tightly, drop heat to the lowest level and simmer for 15 to 20 minutes. With out lifting the lid.

My Photo/07

Cheddar Green Bean Bake

Place 1 cup oat groats covered with water over night, rinsed and drain. Add 1 cup chicken broth, and 1 cup water in a heavy bottomed saucepan and bring to a boil. Reduce heat and simmer gently until groats are tender and the liquid has absorbed.

In another saucepan place 2 cups green beans cut in 1 inch pieces in a streamer basket, cover and steam for 5 minutes until tender. Preheat oven to 375. Saute 2 cups chopped celery, 1/4 cup chopped onions, and 1/2 tsp. celery seed in 2 tb. olive oil in a skillet for 4 minutes, stirring frequently. Add the oats and stir for 1 minute to heat. Add the beans and 3/4 cup of 1 cup cheddar cheese to the oat mixture.

Transfer to a casserole dish. Sprinkle with cracker crumbs and remaining cheese. Bake for 15 minutes or until bubbly.

Stuffed Cabbage

Cook 8 cabbage leaves and 1/2 cup water in a large pot on high until soft. Beat 2 egg whites in a large bowl. Add 1 lb. lean ground beef, 3/4 cup oat bran, 2 tb. milk and 1/8 tsp. black pepper and mix well. Place 2 tb. beef mixture on each cabbage leaf. Fold sides of leaves over the filling and roll, place seam sides down in a casserole dish. Stir 2 cups canned stewed tomatoes, 2 cloves minced garlic and 1 tsp. paprika together in a bowl and pour over cabbage leaves. Cover and cook in a preheated oven at 350 for 45 minutes or until cooked through.

My Photo/08

English Meat Pie

In a heavy frying pan saute 1 cup chopped onions in oil until transparent add 1 lb. lean round steak, and 1 lb. lean pork cut in 3/4 inch cubes. Sear to brown, sprinkle 1 tb. flour over meat and stir in. Add 1/2 lb. small mushrooms cleaned and halved, salt and pepper to taste. Add 1 10 oz. can consomme and 1 1/4 cup boiling water, simmer for 15 to 30 minutes. Roll out a pie crust on a floured board to 1/4 inch thick, fit in a casserole dish. Pour filling into casserole dish. Roll remaining dough to fit top making a gash in the centre. Seal dough with finger tips. Brush top with a mixture of 1 egg yolk with 1 tsp water. Bake at 425 for 15 minutes, reduce heat to 350 for 1/2 hour reduce heat again to 250 and bake for 1 1/2 hours. serves 6 to 8.

157

My Photo

Buffalo Stew

Mix 1 lb. of cubed buffalo or beef with salt and pepper. Brown in a large skillet with 3 to 4 tb. of oil. Add 2 medium size cubed potatoes, 2 chopped carrots, 2 celery sticks chopped and 1 small chopped onion. Add a mixture of chicken and beef broth and simmer in the oven at 350 for 1 1/2 to 2 hours. Add 1 cup frozen peas and a flour and water mixture to thicken. Serve with biscuits .

My Photos/09

Vegan Haggis

Preheat oven to 375. Place 1/2 cup oatmeal in a bowl, preferably the pinhead is variety preferred. Cover with water and let stand for 1 hour, drain thoroughly. Place 2/3 cup brown or green lentils in a pan of water and boil rapidly for 20 minutes or until soft. Drain and rinse in a sieve.

Saute 1 chopped onion in 1 tb. oil, add 2 large grated carrots and 4 to 6 sliced mushrooms, cook for 4 to 5 minutes. Then add 1 tsp.spice choose with a combination of cumin, turmeric, paprika or nutmeg to taste. Add 1 tb. soy sauce, 1 can kidney beans drained and rinsed, 2 cloves of minced garlic. Puree with a sieve or blender to make a thick paste, add water so it's not too thick. Add to the lentil and vegetable mixture. Finally, add the drained oatmeal, salt and pepper to taste, add margarine if it looks too dry. Transfer to a casserole dish and bake for 30 to 40 minutes.

159

My Photos/09

Farmhouse Casserole

In a large skillet brown 3 lb. ground beef well with 2 tb. oil. Add 1 8oz. can mushrooms, 3 to 4 peeled and diced carrots, 1 can drained red kidney beans, 2 13 oz. cans stewed tomatoes and 1 chopped onion. Simmer in the sauce. Spoon into a large casserole dish, cover and cook in the oven at 375 for 1 1/2 hours.

Meanwhile, rub lightly together 1 cup self-raising flour, 1/2 tsp.salt, 1 tsp. baking powder and 4 tb. beef suet or margarine until crumbly. Combine enough cold water to make a soft ball of dough. Pull clumps off to make 12 balls. Arrange on top of the casserole, cook in the oven for another 30 minutes uncovered until golden brown.

My Photo/ 09

Baked Black or Kidney Beans

Preheat oven at 350. Combine 4 cups cooked or canned black or kidney beans, 1 cup thinly sliced celery, 1 red pepper cut very fine, 1/2 cup finely chopped cooked ham, 1 10 oz. can condensed cream of celery soup, 1 cup sour cream, 1 tsp. dry mustard, 1 tb. brown sugar, and 1 1/2 tsp. salt in a bean pot or a deep casserole dish. Bake for 30 minutes uncovered or until slightly browned on top.

My Photo/09

Swedish Meat Balls

In a large bowl beat 2 eggs, stir in 1 cup light cream. Add 1/2 cup dry bread crumbs, let soften for 5 minutes. Cook 1 peeled and thinly chopped onion in a large skillet in 1 tb. butter until tender. Add egg mixture to 1 lb. ground beef and 1/2 lb. ground pork. Season with 1/8 tsp. ground allspice, 1 tb. salt 1/2 tsp. pepper, mix well. Shape into balls lightly. Melt 2 tb. butter in a skillet. Brown meat balls lightly. Add 2 cups hot water and cover and bring to a boil, lower heat and simmer for 20 minutes. Remove meat balls and keep warm. Skim off any fat and strain for a clear liquid, add 1 to tb. of bouillon powder. Blend 2 tb. flour to 4 tb. water in a jar with a tight lid and shake until well mixed. Then stir into skillet until thickened and smooth. Add water if mixture thickens to much Let boil 2 to 3 minutes stirring constantly. Add meat balls and serve when heated evenly.

162

My Photo/08

Baked Fish Dinner In 40 Minute

Preheat oven to 425. Spread 2 lb. frozen halibut steaks in foil lined dish, mix 1/4 cup evaporated milk with 2 tb. steak sauce and spread over fish. Sprinkle with 3/4 cup crushed crackers. Dry 6 small unpeeled, washed, and quartered potatoes dipped in olive oil. Sprinkle with salt generously and arrange in a second baking dish. Remove the packages from 2 10 oz. boxes of frozen mixed vegetables and place on a double thickness of foil. Sprinkle with salt and top with 2 tb. butter. Wrap all separately air tight. Set vegetables and potatoes in oven and bake 15 minutes. Turn over. Place fish in oven continue baking 25 minutes. Serve while hot.

My Photo/09

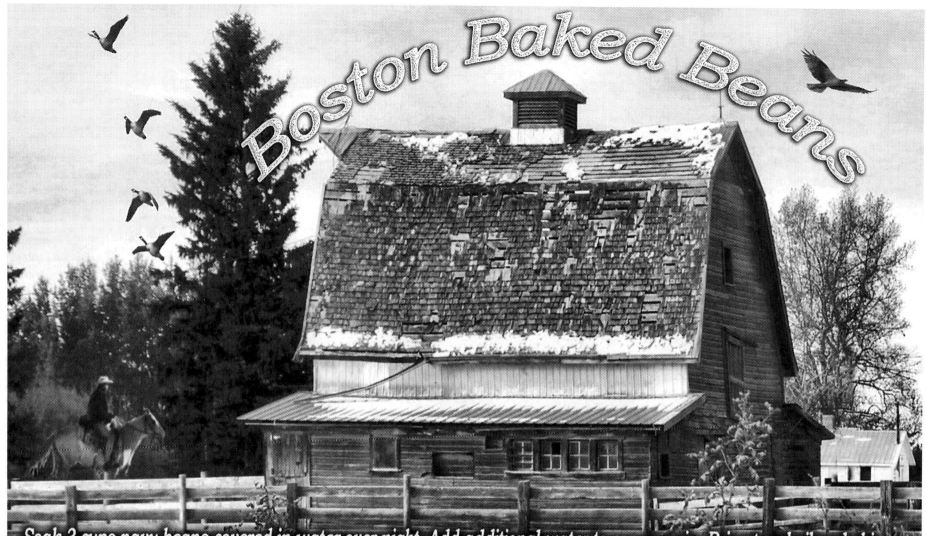

Boston Baked Beans

Soak 3 cups navy beans covered in water over night. Add additional water to cover again. Bring to a boil and skim. Simmer until tender. Add 1/2 lb. salt pork chopped in chunks in an earthenware or an casserole dish with a tight lid. Add 1 small chopped onion, 2 cups boiling water, 1/2 cup dark molasses, 2 tsp. salt. 1 tsp. dry mustard and 1/3 cup brown sugar, mix together evenly. Bake in a very slow oven at 250 for 5 to 6 hours or until beans are soft and tender. Every 1/2 hour replace boiling water that has been absorbed, the last 1/2 hour leave pot uncovered.

164

My Photo/09

Country Captain

Combine 1/4 cup flour, salt and pepper to taste. Cut a 3 to 4 lb. frying chicken in sections, roll in the flour. In a large roaster melt in 1/4 cup shortening. Brown chicken on all sides. Add shortening to a freshly cleaned roaster with a lid and combine 2 chopped onions, 2 chopped green peppers and 1 crushed clove of garlic stirring constantly. Add 3 cups canned tomatoes, 1 tb. chopped parsley. Season with 2 tsp. curry powder, 1/2 tsp. thyme, 1 tsp. salt and 1/2 tsp. pepper. When hot add medium white wine just enough to bring liquid not quite to the top of the chicken pieces. Add 2 cups rice. Cover and bake in a 350 oven for 45 minutes or until chicken is tender and rice has cooked. Place chicken in the center of a platter, arrange a circle of hot cooked rice.

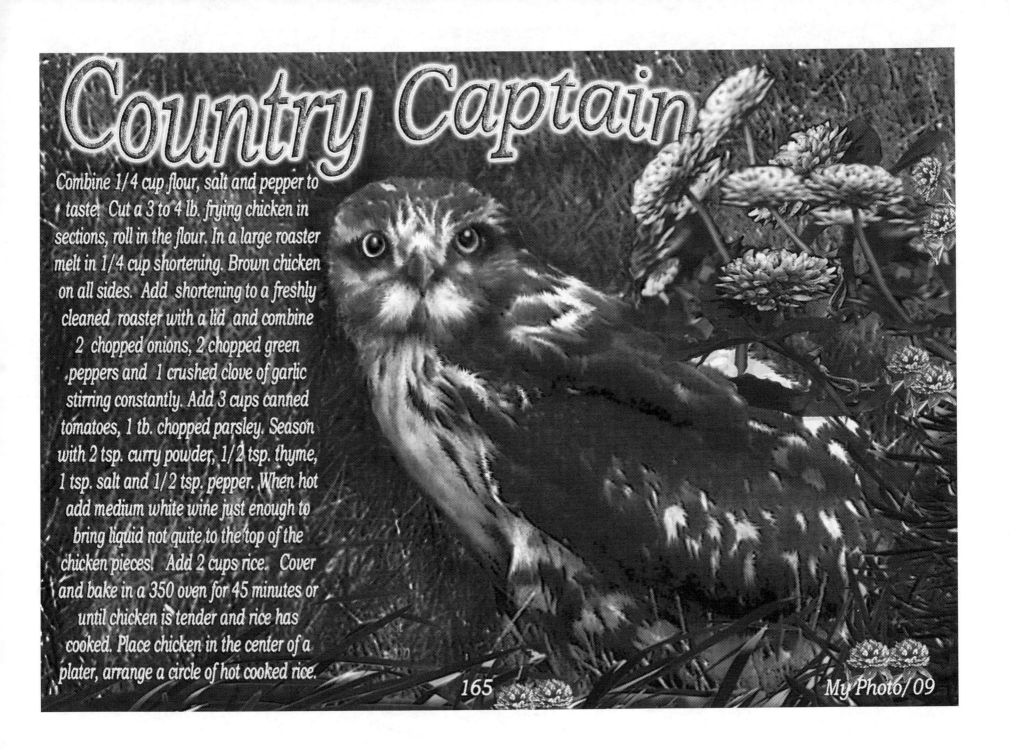

My Photo/09

Homestead Pot Roast

Cut 6 gashes in a 4 to 6 lb round roast of beef or game meat. Insert a clove of garlic in each gash, rub in salt and pepper. Heat 3 tb. oil or bacon fat with 2 tb. butter in a skillet. Add meat and brown quickly on all sides and remove. Add 2 cups sliced onions, 2 cups chopped celery, 1 4 oz. can tomatoes, 1/2 cup sliced green peppers, 2 bay leaves and 2 pinches of oregano. Mix lightly and cook for 10 minutes. Add 3 cut cloves of garlic in roasting pan, place meat on top and cover with vegetables. Add 1 cup boiling water. Cover. Roast slowly at 300 for 3 to 4 hours or until tender.

Swiss Steak

Place 3 lb. round steak cut 1 inch thick on a board. Sprinkle with half of the combined 1/2 cup flour and 1 tsp. salt on one side, pound with a meat mallet hammer for 1 minute. Turn over, sprinkle with remaining flour and pound again for another 1 minute. In a heavy skillet heat 1/4 cup oil or bacon drippings and add the meat, brown on each side. Add 1/4 cup chopped onions, cook for 1 minute. then add 1/4 cup chopped celery and 1/2 cup green pepper sliced. Add 1 can of 13 oz. tomatoes. Cover pan, reduce heat and cook slowly for 1 1/2 hours. If liquid reduces too much add a small can tomato juice.

My Photo/09

Chicken Casserole

Place 1 4 to 5 lb. stewing chicken, 1 sliced carrot, 1 onion quartered and 1 1/2 tsp. salt in a deep kettle. Cover with water, bring to a boil. Simmer covered, about 3 to 4 hours or until tender. Remove chicken, when cooled remove skin and meat from bones. Strain broth, refrigerate meat and broth until ready to prepare casserole.

The next day saute 1 medium onion and 2 large stalks celery with tops finely chopped, in 1/4 cup chicken fat from the top of stock for 5 minutes. Add 6 tb. chicken stock, 1 tsp. sage or poultry seasoning, 1 tsp. salt and pepper. Add to 4 cups soft bread crumbs, mix lightly and set aside.

If needed add butter to chicken fat to make 1 cup. Melt in a large skillet. Add 1 cup flour gradually, 2 tsp. salt, blend until smooth. Stir in 5 cups broth gradually, stir until thickened with no lumps. Remove from heat and cool slightly. Stir a little of the mixture into 4 beaten eggs, then combine the rest of the mixture.

Place stuffing in a greased 4 qt. casserole dish. Cover stuffing with 1/4 cup sauce. Add a layer chicken, cover with remaining sauce. Sprinkle with a mixture of 1 cup dry bread crumbs and 1/4 cup butter. Bake at 375 for 30 minutes, or until browned.

167

My Photo/09

Seasoned Salmon Patties

Mash potatoes with no milk to make 3/4 cup and cool. Mash 2 cans of salmon crushing all lumps or remove any bones. Add the mashed potatoes, 1 egg, 1 tb. Honey mustard, 2 tb. chopped fresh dill, 2 green onions thinly sliced, 1 tsp. salt and 1/4 tsp. pepper. Blend until smooth with some texture. Form into 6 patties and place in a dish of cornmeal and cover on all sides. Heat 1 tb. vegetable oil in a non stick skillet set on medium heat. Cook 4 minutes on each side until golden brown and cooked through. Remove patties and repeat with remaining patties.

Whisk 1/2 cup mayo, 1 tb. Dijon mustard, 1 tb. freshly squeezed lemon juice, 1 tb. vinegar, 3/4 tsp. dried tarragon and 1/2 tsp. sugar together until smooth. Season with salt and pepper. Pour over hot fish patties before serving.

Garry's Photo/ 09

Easy Family Dinner

In a skillet fry 1 lb. lean ground beef with 1 small chopped onion, 1 stock celery and 1/2 red pepper chopped in 1/4 inch squares. Add 1 cup cooked macaroni, mix together well. Then add 1 can tomato soup and 1 small can of stewed tomatoes, salt and pepper to taste. Pour into a casserole dish. Bake for 25 to 30 minutes in a 350 oven and serve hot.

Cindy's Flower/ My Graphics

Onion Herbed Casserole

Peel 2 lb. onions and slice 1/4 inch thick. Combine 1 tsp. salt, 1/4 tsp. Pepper, 1 tsp. paprika, 1 tsp. celery seed, 1/4 tsp.basil. Place layers of onion in a shallow greased casserole, sprinkle seasonings between layers. Add 1/2 cup consomme over casserole and bake at 350 for 45 minutes or until tender. Remove cover and sprinkle 1 cup crushed potato chips over onions, and bake another 10 minutes until crisp and browned.

170

My Photo/08

Sweet Potato Mushroom Casserole

171

Nic's Photos/08

Preheat oven to 350. Heat 1 tb. oil in a skillet to medium heat. Add 1 large finely chopped onion. Cook, stirring often, for 4 to 5 minutes. Increase heat to medium high and add 3 cups chopped mushrooms, stir often while cooking until browned. Stir in 1 tsp. dried thyme, 1 cup light cream, add 1/2 tsp. salt and pepper. Butter a casserole dish and layer 3 sweet potatoes peeled and sliced very thin, alternating with mushroom mixture. Press down with a smaller plate to compress. Pour over cream mixture and cover and bake for 20 minutes. Remove lid and sprinkle 1/2 cup shredded cheese evenly over top. Bake for 35 to 40 minutes or until potatoes are tender.

Tarragon Chicken

Start with 1 3 lb. frying chicken cut in pieces, dredge in flour to coat. Melt 2 tb. butter in a skillet and brown chicken lightly. Add 3/4 cup of white wine, 1/2 cup chicken broth, 1 tsp. dried tarragon. Cover and cook slowly for 40 minutes on low heat or until cooked through and tender. Stir in 1/2 cup light cream with 2 tb. butter and stir to mix in evenly.

172

My photo/08

Whole Wheat Harvest Spaghetti

Cook whole wheat spaghetti to pkg. directions. Saute 1 small chopped red onion, 2 minced garlic cloves., 1 yellow pepper cut in strips and 1 cup sugar snap peas in 2 tb. olive oil for 3 to 4 minutes. Whisk together 1 tb. cornstarch and 1 cup chicken stock, stir into vegetable mixture, cook just until thickened. Toss with hot spaghetti.

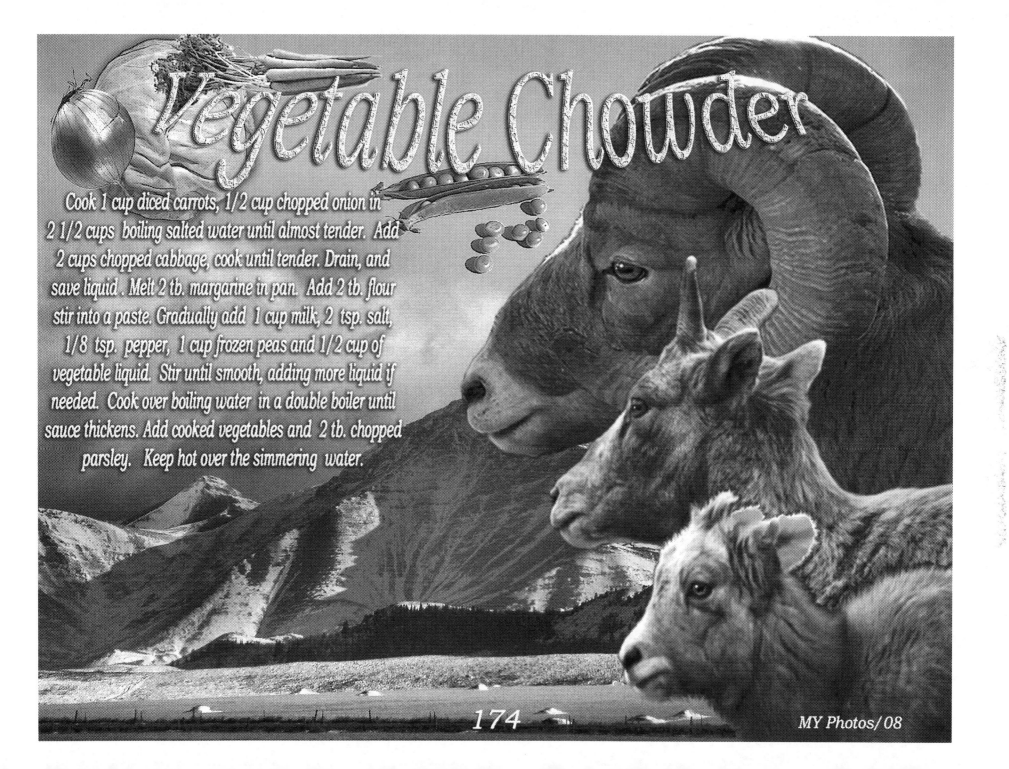

Vegetable Chowder

Cook 1 cup diced carrots, 1/2 cup chopped onion in 2 1/2 cups boiling salted water until almost tender. Add 2 cups chopped cabbage, cook until tender. Drain, and save liquid . Melt 2 tb. margarine in pan. Add 2 tb. flour stir into a paste. Gradually add 1 cup milk, 2 tsp. salt, 1/8 tsp. pepper, 1 cup frozen peas and 1/2 cup of vegetable liquid. Stir until smooth, adding more liquid if needed. Cook over boiling water in a double boiler until sauce thickens. Add cooked vegetables and 2 tb. chopped parsley. Keep hot over the simmering water.

MY Photos/ 08

Italian Style Mini Meat Loaves

Preheat oven to 375. Oil a 6 well muffin tin. Crumble 2 slices Italian whole wheat bread. 2 slices Italian white bread in a mixing bowl. Pour 1 cup water over and let bread soak and mash with fork . Combine with 1 lb. lean ground beef and 1 small finely chopped onion. Then mix in 4 sprigs parsley, 3 tb. grated Parmesan cheese. Mix with fork to blend. Add 1 egg, 1 tsp. salt, 1/4 tsp. pepper. Mix evenly. Shape into the muffin tin 3/4 up and add dabs of butter on each top. Bake for 20 minutes. Pour tomato sauce over each mini loaf and sprinkle with oregano. Bake for another 20 minutes. Makes 6 servings.

My Photos/08

175

Celery Mac and Cheese Loaf

Saute 1/2 cup chopped celery, 2 tb. chopped onion in 2 tb. margarine until tender. Remove from heat, stir in 3 cups cooked elbow macaroni, 1 10oz. can cream of celery soup, 1/2 cup milk and 1 beaten egg. Alternate layers of macaroni mixture and 1 1/2 cups grated cheese in a greased loaf pan ending with cheese. Cover with foil and set in a pan of hot water. Bake at 350 for 1 hour or until loaf has set through.

~ My Photos

176

Easy Breezy Brunswick Stew

Cut 3 cups of left over meats into bite size pieces, set aside. In a saucepan combine 1 10 oz. can consomme with 1 can tomatoes. Bring to a boil. Season with 3 tb. chicken broth , salt and pepper to taste. Add 3 to 4 peeled potatoes chopped into chunks, cook just until tender. Then add meat and 1 pkg. frozen lima beans, 1 cup frozen kernel corn, 1 cup frozen peas and 1 can pearl onions. Simmer until heated through.

My Photo/ Tore down/ 10

Chinese Fried Rice

Rice

Use a measuring cup and add 1 cup rice to 2 cups water. Place rice and cold water in a sauce pan with salt and a tb. margarine with a tight lid. Bring to a boil, stir briskly with a fork, add lid and lower heat and simmer gently for 15 minutes. Water should be absorbed when cooked, but not sticky.

Melt 1/2 cup butter or margarine in a large skillet, add 3 slightly beaten eggs, cook until firm but not hard, stirring with a fork. Add 3 cups cooked rice and cook for 5 minutes, stirring constantly. Then add 1 1/2 cups cooked and diced chicken, ham, pork or shrimp and cook for 10 minutes. Add 2 tb. butter if mixture seems dry. Serve while hot in a rice bowl.

178

Garrys Photo/09

Hot pot

Remove any fat from 1 1/2 lb. lean beef and cut into cubes. Cut 2 carrots and 1 onion into slices. Place into a large skillet with 3 tb. oil and brown evenly on all sides. Remove vegetables and beef set aside. Pour in 1 cup beef broth and bring to a boil. Thicken with a flour and water mixture and simmer for 2 to 3 minutes.

Peel and cut 4 potatoes into slices. Starting and ending with potatoes, neatly arrange the meat, onions, carrots and potatoes in layers in a casserole dish and season with salt and pepper. Pour the gravey over it all to 3/4 fill . adding more later if the dish appears to be dry. Cover and bake in a 350 oven for 2 hours. Uncover 1/2 hour before serving so the top layer of potatoes are browned. serve hot.

179

My Photo/08

Chili Con Carne

Melt 2 tb. butter in a large skillet. Add 1 shredded onion and 1 4 oz. can pimientos. Mix and cook just until onions begin to brown. Add 2 lb. ground beef, stir and cook evenly, about 10 minutes. Add 1 can chopped tomatoes, 2 cups beef stock. Season with 1 tb.chilli powder, 1 tsp. sugar 1 tsp. salt and 1/4 tsp. pepper. Add 3 cans kidney beans. Cover and simmer for 1 hour on low heat.

My Photo/08

Scalloped Ham and Noodle

Cook 1/2 of a 4 oz. pkg.of broad
noodles as directed on package.
Drain and rinse with cold water. Chop
1 cup mushrooms, saute in 2 tb. butter.
Combine noodles, 2 cups diced ham,
2 tsp.mustard with 2 cups white sauce
in a greased casserole. Mix 1 cup
finely grated cheese with 3 tb. fine
bread crumbs and sprinkle on top.
Bake at 350 for 20 to 30 minutes.

181

English Cottage Pie

Preheat oven to 400. Place 4 peeled and diced potatoes in a pan, add water just over the potatoes. Cover and bring to boil on high heat. Drop the heat to medium, cook until tender. Place a skillet over medium heat. Crumble in 1 lb. ground beef and saute for 1 minute. Add 1 diced onion, 2 peeled and diced carrots, continue cooking until meat is no longer pink and onion has browned slightly. Mix in 2 tb. flour evenly. Season with 1/2 tsp. cinnamon, 1 tb. Italian season, 2 tb. chopped parsley. In a small bowl, combine 1 1/2 cups beef broth and 1 tb. tomato paste. mix together. Add to meat mixture and salt and pepper to taste. Lower heat and simmer for 15 minutes, stir occasionally, until most of the liquid has absorbed. Spoon mixture into a pie plate. Mash drained and cooked potatoes until smooth, add a little butter and milk, whip until fluffy. Salt and pepper to taste. Spoon on top and spread over beef filling evenly. Sprinkle 1/2 cup of shredded cheddar cheese on top. Bake for 25 minutes. until brown and cheese has melted.

My Photo/08

Bubble and Squeak

The name bubbles and squeak comes from a English dish which is used as a way to use up left overs from a roast dinner, that squeaks when the potato bubbles break.

Heat some oil in a frying pan and add thin slices of left over cold roast, fry quickly on both sides until lightly browned. Remove and keep hot. Fry 1 small shredded onion until browned. Add 2 cups cold mashed potatoes and cold greens of any kind and mixed together. Season to taste. Stir until thoroughly hot and turn out on to a hot dish. Place the meat on top and serve.

My Photo/ 09

Italian Bean and Sausage

Heat 2 tsp. oil in a skillet, add 5 oz. sausage links and cook over medium high heat. Stir occasionally until browned on all sides, remove from skillet and set aside. In the skillet combine 1/2 cup diced onion, and 1 minced clove of garlic, stirring occasionally, until onions are translucent. Add 1 cup drained canned chopped Italian tomatoes, and 1 4 oz. can of white kidney beans, drained. Season with 1 tsp. chopped basil, salt and pepper and stir to combine. Reduce heat to low and simmer to blend. Slice sausage thinly and add to bean mixture, cook until heated. through serves 2.

184

Salisbury Steak

Chop 4 strips bacon and mix in 1 1/2 lb. ground beef, 1/2 lb. ground pork. 2 tb. chopped onion, 1 tb. minced green pepper, 1 tsp. chopped parsley, 1 tsp. salt, 1/2 tsp. pepper. Shape into large patty cakes. Place 3 inches under a broiler heat. Broil 12 minutes, turn once.

Steak and Kidney Pie

Cut 1 1/2 lb. steak and 1/2 lb. kidney into 1/2 inch cubes and dredge in flour that has been seasoned with salt and pepper. Arrange meat in a greased casserole dish and add 1 tb. chopped onion, 1 tsp. chopped parsley, 1/2 lb. sliced mushrooms and just enough beef stock to cover meat. Cover and cook in a moderate 350 oven for 1 hour or until meat is tender. Remove cover and replace it with pastry. Prick with a fork to allow steam to escape. Return to oven, bake at 450 for 15 minutes or until browned.

186

Cindy's Photo/07

Quiche Lorraine

Beat together 2 eggs, 1/2 cup milk, 1/2 cup mayonnaise and 1 tb.corn starch. Fold in 1/4 cup diced ham, 1/4 cup diced tomato, 1/4 cup chopped onion, 1/4 cup chopped mushrooms and 1/2 cup grated cheddar cheese. Pour into an unbaked pie shell. Sprinkle 1 cup grated cheddar cheese on top. Bake in a preheated 350 oven for 25 to 30 minutes or until golden brown and firm to the touch in the middle.

My Photo/ 10

Spaghetti and Meat Sauce

Brown 1 lb. hamburger until cooked through. Drop the heat, add 1 finely chopped onion, 1 finely chopped stick celery, 1 small seeded and chopped red pepper, 1/2 cup red cooking wine, 1 tsp. wine vinegar, 1 14 oz. can plum tomatoes chopped with juice while in the can. Mix together evenly. Season with salt and pepper. Then add 2 to 3 finely chopped cloves garlic, 3 tb. finely chopped fresh parsley, 1 piece dried chilli chopped. Stir to mix together evenly, raise the heat to medium high, bring to a boil and cook for about 5 minutes. Lower the heat, cover and simmer until vegetables are soft, about 30 minutes.

Nic's Photo /07

Pasta Dough

Place 2 cups flour in the centre of a clean smooth work surface. Make a well in the middle. Break 4 eggs into the well. Add a pinch of salt. Start beating the eggs with a fork, gradually drawing the flour from the inside walls of the well. As the paste thickens, continue the mixing with your hands. Incorporate as much flour as you can, until the mixture forms into a mass, it will still be lumpy. If still too sticky add more flour to your hands and to the dough. Set the dough to the side, and scrape off all traces of the leftover until the surface is dough free. Wash and dry hands. Lightly flour the work surface. Knead the dough until smooth and elastic. Cut dough in half. Flour the rolling pin and the work surface, pat the dough down. Roll the dough out to a paper thin flat circle. Repeat for the second dough. Roll dough as you would a cinnamon roll. Then cut the noodles any thickness you like. Cook pasta in a large amount of rapidly boiling salted water. Drop pasta into the water all at once using a wooding spoon. Stir while cooking for about 25 minutes, or until tender. Pour into a colander in a sink, toss with butter and serve with sauce.

My Blue Jay/ 09

Cowboys Chili

Cook 2 lb. ground beef in a large Dutch oven, add 1 cup chopped onions, 1 cup chopped green peppers, 2 minced cloves garlic and 3 tb. chili powder in 1 tb. oil until meat has lost its pink color. Add 1 can undrained tomatoes, 1 medium size zucchini cut into 1 inch chunks, 1/2 cup tomato paste, 1 1/2 tsp. salt, 1 19 oz. can red kidney beans and 1 12 oz. can whole kernel corn. Cooked covered and simmer until zucchini is tender.

189

My Photos

Birds in Nest

Melt 3 tb. margarine, blend in 1 1/2 tb. flour and salt and pepper. Blend in 1 cup chicken stock , stirring over medium until thickened. Add 2 cups of cooked diced chicken, mix together until chicken has heated through. Place onto a serving plate with a egg noodle ring that has been plated for serving. Place chicken mixture in centre of ring.

Shake and Bake

In a bowl mix 1/2 cup bread crumbs, season with 2 tsp. curry, 1/2 tsp.dry mustard, 1/4 tsp. paprika, 2 tsp. onion powder, 1/4 tsp. garlic powder, 3/4 tsp.salt and 1/4 tsp.pepper. Mix well and shake to coat meat. Great for chicken

191

Garry's Photos/ 10

Stuffed Cheese Manicotti

In a large skillet heat 1 tsp. olive oil. Saute 3 crushed cloves garlic until golden brown about 2 minutes. Stir in 3 8 oz. cans tomato sauce, 1 tb. Italian seasoning, 1/4 tsp. ground pepper, bring to a boil. Reduce heat and cover and simmer, stir occasionally for about 15 minutes. Preheat oven to 300. Grease a 9x13 baking dish. In a medium bowl, combine 1 1/2 cups part skim ricotta cheese, 1 1/4 cups shredded mozzarella cheese and 3/4 cup grated Parmesan cheese Add 1 lightly beaten egg and 1/4 cup chopped flat leaf parsley. Fill the manicotti shells with the cheese mixture. Place in the baking dish. Pour the sauce over the shells. Bake until browned and bubbling, 30 to 40 minutes.

192

Garry's Photo/09

Savory Ham Pie

Saute 3 tb. chopped onion, 1/4 cup chopped green pepper in 1/4 cup margarine. Stir in 6 tb. flour and make a paste, add 1 10 oz. can condensed chicken soup, 1 1/3 cups milk, cook until thickened. Add 1 1/2 cups diced cooked ham, 1 tb. lemon juice. Mix well and pour into a greased baking dish.

Roll out a biscuit dough on a floured board, cut with a doughnut cutter and arrange on top of ham mixture. Preheat oven to 450, bake 15 minutes, reduce heat to 425 and bake 10 minutes longer.

My Photos and graphics

Country Style Chicken

Wash a 3 lb. chicken and wipe dry with paper towel. Mix 1/2 tsp. of salt with 1/2 cup flour and roll chicken in mixture. Melt 6 tb. margarine in a frying pan and brown the chicken on all sides on a medium high heat for about 10 minutes. Peel 6 medium potatoes and cut in half. Peel and quarter 6 medium onions, peel 6 medium carrots and quarter lengthwise, cut and seed 2 green peppers into 1/2 inch strips. Season with 1 tb. sugar, 1 tsp. salt and 1/4 tsp. pepper. Add 2 crushed cloves of garlic. Place 2/3 of the vegetables in bottom of a large kettle. Place chicken on top and add remaining vegetables. Pour 2 1/2 cups canned stewed tomatoes and 3 cups boiling water over all. Cover tightly and bring to a boil. Reduce heat and let simmer until tender, about 1 1/2 to 2 hours.

194

Garry's Photo/06

Russia with Love Potato Patties

Peel 3 lb. potatoes and boil with 1 bay leaf and 1 clove of garlic until soft. Remove bay leaf and mash and cool. Mix in 3 eggs completely. Add 6 to 7 tb. wheat flour, salt and pepper to taste, let stand 10 to 15 minutes.

Filling

Chop 1/2 medium head cabbage, 1 large onion, peel and grate 1 carrot. Place in a frying pan with 2 tb. olive oil, cover and cook on medium heat until cabbage has become tender. Add 1 small can champagne mushrooms and 1 to 2 tb. Vegeta seasoning. Continue frying uncovered, mixing occasionally, until liquid completely evaporates, remove from heat and cool.

Sprinkle flour on a board. Make a flat potato patty 1/4 inch thick and 3 inches in diameter. Place 1 to 2 tsp. of filling in the center of the patty and close up the edges tightly around the filling. Turn upside down and make into a thick and flat round patty gently. Preheat a nonstick frying pan. Fry patties in olive oil on medium heat for 5 to 6 minutes on each side until golden brown. Serve with sour cream.

195

Nic's Photo/09

Meat and Vegetable Pie

Brown 1 1/2 lbs. steak cut in 1 inch cubes in 2 tb. butter with 1/2 cup chopped onions, 1 cup chopped celery, 1 cup chopped carrots, 2 small potatoes chopped. Add salt and pepper to taste. Cook on medium low for 25 minutes until meat and vegetables are slightly browned Add three cups water, simmer to capture all browning. Add 2 tb. beef broth powder and simmer to dissolve, taste, season more if needed. Add frozen peas. Thicken with 2 tb. uncooked oatmeal and simmer until slightly thickened. Set aside

Topping................2 cups flour, 1 tsp. salt, cut in 2/3 cup shorting until crumbly, Add 6 tb. to 8 tb. cold water gradually just enough to form a pastry ball. Wrap in plastic and form a firm ball and cool for 30 to 35 minutes. Can be made ahead of time. Roll out and line a pie plate with pastry. Pour in the stew just enough to fill. Top with remaining pastry. If any is left over freeze

My Photos

196

A cowboy is an animal herder who takes care of horses and cattle on a ranch. The word cowboy dates back to 1725 in the English language. Cowboys are also referred to as wranglers. The American cowboy of the late 19th century arose from northern Mexico and many became a legend in the rodeo industry. The cowboy has roots tracing back to Spain and the early settlers of the Americas. There are also cattle workers in many parts of the world, through South America and Australia, who work the same tasks as cowboys. For those as young as 12 or 13 who had the physical ability and the necessary skills. Often began their careers as adolescents and might handle cows and horses for the rest of his or her life.

John B Stetson was the son of a Philadelphia hat maker. Heading west for a warmer and dryer climate in 1862, John began working on a animal hides. He used his hands to work the hide in a kneading motion much as in bread dough. He would dip the hide in boiling water for some time, repeating this many times. He shaped the piece into a hat letting it dry and harden, it had a rather tall crown and wide brim.

He soon found it to be a very good protector from sun and rain. John sold his first hat for $5.00.

My Photos/09
My and Nic Graphics

197

" If you don't
know where
you are going,
any road will
get you there.

Lewis Carroll

Order this book online at www.trafford.com
or email orders@trafford.com

Most Trafford titles are also available at major online book retailers.

Note for Librarians: A cataloguing record for this book is available from Library
and Archives Canada at www.collectionscanada.ca/amicus/index-e.html

Printed in the United States of America.

ISBN: 978-1-4269-3497-1 (sc)

*Our mission is to efficiently provide the world's finest, most comprehensive book publishing
service, enabling every author to experience success. To find out how to publish your book, your
way, and have it available worldwide, visit us online at www.trafford.com*

Trafford rev. 8/09/2010

www.trafford.com

North America & international
toll-free: 1 888 232 4444 (USA & Canada)
phone: 250 383 6864 ♦ fax: 812 355 4082